I0148260

HOLY WEEK IN TOMÉ

A NEW MEXICO PASSION PLAY

Translated by
Thomas J. Steele, S.J.

SUNSTONE
PRESS
SANTA FE

Copyright©1976 by the Immaculate Conception Parish,
Tomé, New Mexico

ALL RIGHTS RESERVED

ISBN - 0 - 913270 - 63 - 6

TABLE OF CONTENTS

Preface

Introduction 5

Text 24

Preface 30

Wednesday of Holy Week 36

Holy Thursday   (1) 42

                       (2)* 60

                       (3) 94

Good Friday   (1) 104

                       (2)* 106

                       (3) 128

                       (4) 152

Holy Saturday 176

Easter Sunday 178

Mr. Otero's Narrative 194

Addenda 201

ILLUSTRATIONS

Iglesia Catolica, Tome, N. Mex. 35

Los Soldados Romanos y Los Judios 62

Jesucristo es prendido 63

Jesucristo en la carcel 93

El Lienzo de la Veronica 123

Nuestra Senora de los Dolores 130

La Sangre de Cristo 131

El Descendimiento 143

El Centurion 150

Nuestro Senor en la urna 151

N.S. Soledád 157

Domingo de Resurreccion 181

"Vista mobile" poster 193

HYMNS

Miserere Mei Deus 38

Vuestro Cuerpo Sacrosanto 44

Pues Padeciste Tan Desolada 46

A Jesus Yo Quiero Acudir 54

Agonizante en el Huerto 64
Pues Padeciste Por Amor 72
Mi Dios y Mi Redentor 82
Venid O Cristianos 104
Acompañemos al Calvario 116
Perdón, O Dios Mío 134
Amante Jesús Mio 146
Venid Almas Devotas 154
Estabas Madre Dolorosa 166
Ayudemos Almas 170
Rex Caelestis, Rex Gloriae 184
Dios Te Salve 184
El Redentor Cristianos, Nos Convida 186

SERMONS

Thu   3 pm   Prendimiento 66
Thu   7 pm   Posentio 96
Fri   9 am   Tres Caidas 126
Fri   3 pm   Descendimiento 140
Fri   7 pm   Soledád 162
Sun   9 am   Resurrección 188

La Sentencia 112, 201

PREFACE

The Spanish of the text of the Passion Play, which makes up the basic document of this volume, is spelled phonetically rather than with dictionary correctness; but since the text exists as a unique document of its sort, it was thought better not to correct it but to leave it as it came into being (with of course correction of simple slips of the typewriter).

I would like to thank Mr. Fred Landavazo, its principal author, for letting me use it as well as the illustrations; Mr. Ben M. Otero, for allowing me to copy and use the Passion Play movie he took; Mr. Edwin Berry, for his generosity with his knowledge, especially of the hymns; and Mr. Ralph C. Castillo, who let me copy and use the movie he took of the ceremonies on the Cerro de Tomé. And I would like to thank Fr. Robert Auman, the present pastor, and commend his predecessors, Frs. Joseph Mueller, Joseph Assenmacher, and especially the great Jean-Baptiste Rallière.

Thanks are also due to Dr. Florence Hawley Ellis, whose article she allowed me to quote so liberally; Professors John Archibeque of the University of Albuquerque and Roger Martin of Regis College, for their help with the Spanish; and my Jesuit brethren and my friends both in Albuquerque and Denver for their support and encouragement.

INTRODUCTION

An image of Christ large as life . . . is paraded through the streets, in the midst of an immense procession, accompanied by a glittering array of carved images, representing the Virgin Mary, Mary Magdalene, and several others; while the most notorious personages of antiquity, who figured at that great era of the World's history,—the centurion with a band of guards, armed with lances, and apparelled in the costume supposed to have been worn in those days,—may be seen bestriding splendidly caparisoned horses, in the breathing reality of flesh and blood.[1]

A stirring description of a stirring ceremony, the passion play enacted every year in the old days by the people of a few towns of New Mexico, including Tomé, a small village about thirty miles south of Albuquerque. Fray Francisco Atanasio Dominguez referred to the Holy Week ceremonies in Tomé in that most interesting year, 1776, Josiah Gregg's words quoted above describe what he may have seen there in the 1830's, Florence Hawley Ellis wrote at length about the Tomé pageant in 1952,[2] and now a lengthy and comprehensive account of the 1946 services and a short but very touching movie of the 1947 enactment have come to light. The account was prepared by Messrs.

Fred Landavazo, Edwin Berry, and Juan Estevan Zamora; the film was made by Mr. Ben M. Otero of the neighboring town of Los Lunas.

In my recent book *Santos and Saints,* I hypothesized that such rites as the Tomé play and the Deposition from the Cross still performed by the people of San Felipe parish in Albuquerque's Old Town form a connective link between the santos—the folk-art pictures and statues of Christ and the angels and saints which were created in New Mexico in the eighteenth and nineteenth centuries—and the ceremonies of the Cofradía de Nuestro Padre Jesús Nazareno, better known as the Penitentes. The purpose of any contemporary holy action or item is to represent the most holy action of the "culture hero" (in Christianity, Christ himself) or to picture some holy person at his or her most powerful. Thus the majority of the santos show the saints in an iconic repose, equivalently in heaven, for in heaven the saint is more powerful than he or she was on earth, and has been commissioned as patron of certain human needs for all subsequent time throughout the whole world. The santos of the mature Christ, on the other hand, show him at his most powerful by representing him in his passion, and therefore these pictures and (especially) statues generally are far more dynamic; the statues are frequently hinged at the shoulders to allow their being moved through the various stages of stripping, scourging, crowning with thorns, robing in different garments, being displayed to the crowd, crucifixion, deposition, and burial. The Penitente brotherhood climaxed the Lenten season by appointing one of their own members to play the part of Christ in a painfully penitential reenactment of the crucifixion, though by tying rather than by nailing. Now since the Tomé passion play uses a statue of Christ to take the main role—the same "image of Christ large as life" to which Gregg referred—and uses other *bultos* to enact other of the important roles, it seems that this painless but highly dynamic ceremonial stands as a link between the mere santos on the one hand and the activities of the Penitentes on the other.[3]

Tomé was originally founded by and named for Tomé (or Thomé) Dominguez de Mendoza in the seventeenth century; after the 1680 Pueblo Rebellion and the Reconquest a dozen years later, none of the Dominguez family (all of whom survived) seem to have chosen to return, so just before the middle of the next century the land was granted to other persons, largely *genizaros* (Indians converted to Christianity and living a Spanish lifestyle). The church there, which was completed by 1750, remained a *visita* of Belén, Isleta, or Albuquerque for many years, but in 1821 acquired a resident pastor.[4]

The Tomé ceremonies, initiated well before the end of the eighteenth century as Fray Dominguez' reference shows, could not have begun under the auspices of the Penitentes, who did not come into being until the last decade of that century or the first of the nineteenth. But as Gregg's description proceeds, it is clear that the influence of the Penitentes asserted itself very powerfully during the early years of the last century:

I once chanced to be in the town of Tomé on Good Friday, when my attention was arrested by a man almost naked, bearing, in imitation of Simon, a huge cross upon his shoulders, which, though constructed of the lightest wood, must have weighed over a hundred pounds. The long end dragged upon the ground, as we have seen it represented in sacred pictures, and about the middle swung a stone of immense dimensions, appended there for the purpose of making the task more laborious. Not far behind followed another equally destitute of clothing, with his whole body wrapped in chains and cords, which seemed buried in the muscles, and which so cramped and confined him that he was scarcely able to keep pace with the procession.[5]

But with the coming of Bishop Lamy and his non-Hispano priests, the Penitentes fell from even the ineffectual intolerance accorded them by Fray Niño de Guevara and Bishop Zubiría. In Tomé it was doubtless during the lengthy regime of Father J.B. Rallière, pastor from 1858 to 1911, that the Penitente influences were almost totally separated from the passion play as it had existed in the eighteenth century and existed later into this era. It may also be suspected that it was the influence of Fr. Rallière that added the celebration of the resurrection to the ceremonies, for indigenous New Mexico Spanish spirituality had tended to focus almost exclusively on the suffering and death of Christ and almost not at all on his resurrection; only two-tenths of one percent of a sample of santos show the risen Christ, but upwards of thirteen percent represent Christ in his passion and death.[6]

On Wednesday evening, the ceremonies began. The first ritual is that of Tinieblas, a New Mexican development of a standard Roman Catholic ceremony during which a number of psalms were chanted in Latin, and after each psalm a sacristan extinguished one candle on a large candelabrum holding thirteen candles. After the last psalm, the sacristan carried the remaining lighted candle out of the sanctuary into the sacristy; this represented the death of Christ, when the scriptures tell us that "there was darkness over all the land . . . and the veil of the temple was rent in twain from the top to the bottom; and the earth did quake; and the rocks were rent" (Matt. 27:45, 51). The people in attendance, upon the disappearance of the candle, clapped their psalters shut and rapped them on the pews a few times to symbolize the world-chaos upon the removal of Christ, the principle of order, from the cosmos: one may speak in church, or sing, but one may not make a racket, except this one time of the year. In New Mexico, this ceremony was elevated to an art form. According to participants, the holy confusion raised at a full-scale Tinieblas was enough to make an impressionable child certain that the world had come to the end—as in a sense it had, of course. The clanking of chains, the chattering of the matracas, the shouts, the total darkness within which invisible shapes moved rapidly around celebrated the passage of Christ, the principle of cosmos, from the world.

After the ceremony, the crucifix still to be seen at the right of the Tomé sanctuary was carried in procession around the village to bless it; this was the same crucifix used as an object of veneration on Holy Thursday, as may be seen in the movie. According to various informants in Tomé, the Wednesday ceremonies were not under the direction of the Cofradía de San José, which moderated the remaining activities. According to one very informed person, in the old days certain Penitentes were permitted to lie in the doorway of the church so that the faithful would have to walk over them to enter; this, I am told, was the only appearance of typically Penitente activity in connection with the Tomé ceremonies during this century, and it disappeared just prior to World War I. Such was the completeness of Father Rallière's reforms since Gregg's visit of the 1830's.

Mr. Otero's film of the passion play covers only the outdoor episodes, though those are the bulk of the ceremonies and the most interesting. The action resumes on Holy Thursday. Since it is a period of mourning bells are not rung, and the parishioners come instead to the sound of matracas whirled by several boys. When the people arrive, the crucifix carried in the previous evening's procession is leaning against the wall of the church—though this is usually indoors, Mr. Otero arranged to have it moved outside so he would be able to film it. Then the townsmen who play the parts of the Jews and the Roman soldiers gather near the church and, under the leadership of the centurion, rush forward to apprehend Christ. The actual capture takes place inside the church, so it does not appear in the movie; but Dr. Ellis' article and Mr. Landavazo's scenario recount what occurs:

> Inside, after the congregation has settled to sing *Agonisante en el huerto* (Agony in the Garden), the priest carries on the story as his sermon. Christ, praying in the garden, is brought a chalice, bitter cup of affliction, by an angel. But as the angel disappears, into the garden come Jews and soldiers (p. 206).
>
> THE PRIEST — Whom seek ye?
> THE JEWS — Jesus of Nazareth, King of the Jews.
> THE PRIEST — (Continuing to read the gospel,[7] then turning to ask) Whom seek ye?
> THE JEWS — Jesus of Nazareth, King of the Jews.
> THE PRIEST — (Turning for the third time to ask) Whom seek ye?
> THE JEWS — Jesus of Nazareth, King of the Jews.
> THE PRIEST — I am he; here I am.
>   Judas places the noose around the neck of the Divine Image and ties his hands [with the loose end].[8]

Three santos of Christ were used in each performance of the total play, one only on Wednesday night and Thursday morning, the "Sangre de Cristo" crucifix, the second a Mexican bulto dating from 1722 and retouched in 1897 which undergoes only the crucifixion and burial, and the third, the Divino Rostro (Divine Image) mentioned

above, which is used for the capture, the way of the cross, and the resurrection.[9] Once this bulto has been captured, there is a procession around the plaza which the movie unfortunately does not show. Then Dr. Ellis continues:

> Upon their return to the church, the congregation finds Christ (the life-size, gaunt Santo Entierro carved from wood and painted by some long-dead *santero* of the area) imprisoned in a little room made of bars. There he is guarded by the Roman soldiers, but three angels appear to sweep the jail, and to offer flowers, perfumes, and incense. Here, with wrists bound around by a chain of rope, Christ remains all night (pp. 206-07).

The Good Friday services, after the usual morning ceremonies associated with the Mass of the Presanctified, are structured upon an ancient Catholic devotion, the Way of the Cross. This was especially fostered by the Franciscan Order, which did all the evangelizing of New Mexico up to the end of the eighteenth century, so it can be expected that the Via Crucis figured prominently in the catechetical methods used with Indians and Spanish alike. Fray Dominguez noted that in 1776 the church at Tomé contained "fourteen old, but not torn, canvases arranged on the whole wall," and it would be tempting to guess that these were the fourteen stations of the Way of the Cross.[10]

The first station occurs at nine in the morning in the front of the church, which represents the palace of Pilate, the Roman governor. He is enthroned on the balcony above the main door, with two soldiers, a serving boy, and Barabbas; the bulto of Christ is carried on a pallet into the churchyard below, and the bultos of Our Lady of Sorrows and Saint John are stationed just outside the church door. The priest prays the prayer of the first station, "Contemplate, my soul, in this first station, what sort of place the palace of Pilate is, where the redeemer of the world was cruelly crowned with thorns and sentenced to death." The Spanish opening words of the prayer, "Contempla, alma, en esta estación, que es el lugar," will remain with only minor changes ("la casa" for "el lugar," for instance) throughout the fourteen stations. The imperative to contemplate the various places along the journey to death and the tomb is a method of drawing the congregation into the action of the death of Christ so that each of the faithful may benefit, by his or her unity with the suffering Lord, from the merits of his saving death. After the prayer, the first station continues; in the words of Mr. Otero's narrative, read as the movie he made was shown:

> When the case was presented, Pilate saw that the accused man was not guilty, and said, "Jesus of Nazareth is innocent; I find no guilt at all in this man." The leader of the Jews cries, "He is an enemy of Caesar, a disturber of public order and a spreader of false teaching."

> After Pilate has let Barabbas go, he washes his hands and says, "I am innocent of the blood of this just man."
>
> And Jesus is condemned to death.[11]

When the chains are removed from Barabbas' wrists and draped over the railing, the criminal rushes through the doorway at the rear that leads into the choirloft and joins the actors below. After Pilate has washed his hands, he reads the proclamation condemning Christ to death and directing that the proclamation be read again as Jesus passes by the courthouse on his way around the Tomé square to the Calvary. Dr. Ellis notes that the document is "signed by that dignitary (Pilate) in the position of 'Presidente' rather than in the old form, 'Roman Procurator.' "[12] Pilate then folds the paper and hands it to one of the Roman soldiers. The centurion urges his fiery horse forward under the balcony and raises his spear to the railing, and the soldier impales the proclamation of death on the point of the lance, which is adorned with a small purple dress mocking Christ's claim to kingship.

The second station is Christ's taking up the cross, and is represented by a man's holding a cross about four feet long over Christ's shoulder; he, or Simon of Cyrene later, holds it there throughout the rest of the procession.

The centurion on horseback leads the people forward on their way around the oval plaza of the town of Tomé. The procession pauses at intervals for the various remaining stations of the cross; the third station is the first fall of Christ under the cross, which is represented by the genuflection of the two men carrying the front of the pallet upon which the bulto of Christ stands. The fourth station is the *Encuentro,* the meeting of Mary with her son, dramatized by four women carrying forward the platform upon which Nuestra Señora de los Dolores stands until the two statues face each other; this is a very poignant moment in the ritual, and one which looks forward to the final and perhaps most moving episode in the entire pageant.

The fifth station is the seriocomic incident of Simon of Cyrene's being forced to help Christ bear the cross. In the movie, he is lurking by a fence-corner when he is seized upon by the Jews and soldiers and dragged forward struggling to the place where the bulto of Christ is.

The next event is Veronica's wiping the face of Jesus with a cloth, upon which the features of his countenance are miraculously preserved. A young lady comes forward holding a piece of light canvas, folded horizontally so that the painting of Christ is hidden from view. As she and the statue of Christ confront one another, she raises the cloth to his face and releases the bottom two corners, presses it around his head, then turns away and displays the image of the savior to the people. In Mr. Otero's narrative, "The woman Veronica, seeing Jesus so tired and with his face covered with perspiration, dust, spittle, and blood from the abuse he received, wipes his face with her veil. Then she shows the cloth to the bystanders with the countenance of the Lord imprinted on it" (p. 3). The painting was done at Father

Rallière's request by one Donato Estrella; it may still be seen in the Tomé museum.[13]

Usually the seventh station is the second fall of Christ, but in the Tomé ceremonies this seems to be transposed with the eighth, the encounter of Jesus with the pious women of Jerusalem. At this point in the movie several women come forward, one of them carrying an infant, and kneel before the Lord. In Mr. Otero's account, they "weep bitterly to see him so badly hurt" (p. 3).

The next two stations are both falls of the weakened Christ; Mr. Otero notes that the first of these occurs, as Pilate's decree suggests, "in front of the door of the courthouse" and that "Jesus has sustained a large and deadly wound in his shoulder" (p. 3). At this time, some man known for his learning rereads Pilate's *Sententia* again. After the third fall, according to the movie, Father Assenmacher, pastor of Tomé from 1939 to 1952, preaches the "sermon on the three falls of Christ and Veronica," as the townspeople commonly refer to it. Father Assenmacher's sermon, interestingly, identifies Veronica with the woman taken in adultery of John 8:3-11.

Noting the sermon, Dr. Ellis remarks that "the Jews and Romans hardly wait for its conclusion to begin gambling for the clothes of Christ" (p. 208). The definite discrepancy among the account by Landavazo, Berry, and Zamora, the movie, and the account by Dr. Ellis seems to stem from a change in setting that she notes:

> ...the people wait in the churchyard in front of the Memorial Monument, a large concrete shell erected by a townsman in honor of the men from Tomé who died in World War II. It is a stage, built specifically for use in the Easter pageant which the village so wants to perpetuate, although nowadays it sometimes is difficult to persuade the young people to agree to take the parts which necessitate—as in the days of the past—repeated practice to attain convincing movement and disregard of spectators during final presentation of the drama.
>
> The choir sings; the Jews and the Romans, who have gathered in a yard at the side of the church, file in; the people wait. And then the priest steps up onto one end of the curtained stage area to tell the old story of Christ's death for the sins of His people, a people neither more nor less sinful than we today. He speaks quietly, simply, in Spanish which still shows a trace of his European background, and the wind ruffles his hair as he tells the congregation that men and women must try again to follow the precepts of good will and good works for which their Savior died so long ago. And then, when he has finished and stepped down, the billowing curtains of the stage front are torn aside and the people fall on their knees before the scene of Calvary.
>
> In the center, against the painted background showing Jerusalem and its hills, is the tall black cross of Christ, with

the lifesize wooden *santo* suspended from it by nails which pass through punctured hands and feet, and with a long purple cloth holding his body against the bar (pp. 208-09).

In the year of the movie, on the other hand, the Memorial Monument was as yet unbuilt, and Mr. Otero's narrative suggests that the action continues unbroken following the end of the sermon:

> Now that the Lord has arrived at Mount Calvary, he is stripped of his garments. They nail him to the cross, and in his agony they offer him to drink wine mixed with myrrh. In accordance with the decree of Pilate, he has been crucified between two thieves, Dismas and Gestas, by both of whom he is consoled until his death.
>
> The Jews dispose of the holy robe of Jesus by casting dice (p. 3).

But until the year before the movie was taken, it seems clear that the crucifixion took place in the afternoon at three o'clock, and that it was staged in the church: "the altar is covered with a black curtain, in front of this is another curtain, this one white." Then after the reading of the tenth, eleventh, and twelfth stations, the Landavazo narrative continues, "Finally, the priest reads the Gospel from the Holy Scriptures. Here the curtain is drawn aside. Jesus Christ is seen nailed to the cross. Mary Most Holy, Saint John, Joseph and Nicodemus, the soldiers, the centurion, blind Longinus and the rest of the Jews stand beneath the cross. They all present a most heart-rending scene, all gazing up at Jesus Christ dead on the cross." The series of changes seems to lie in this, that with the completion of the Memorial, the leaders of the pageant were again able to stage the highly effective revelation of so striking a theatrical tableau, and consequently, the story was carried forward mainly by Fr. Assenmacher's narration, as it had been in the past, rather than by dramatization; and when the curtains were opened either in the church or at the Memorial Monument, Christ and the two thieves were already on the crosses. On the other hand, in the 1947 performance shown in the movie, the stripping of Christ had been followed by the positioning of his "living" body on the cross, and then by extensive enactment of the reviling by the Jews and the soldiers, the raising of the sponge of wine to Christ's lips (shown twice in the movie), and the gambling for his garments while he was hanging on the cross. It must be concluded that neither Dr. Ellis' nor Mr. Landavazo's account is in error, but that we have instead a case of the "notwithstanding some changes" that both Mr. Landavazo and Mr. Otero mention.

Dr. Ellis notes that at the deposition of the bodies

> The boys, too, are carefully lowered from their crosses, and fall with proper limpness over the shoulders of men who deposit them in the trench behind a low front wall which permits unobserved exit (pp. 209-10).

12

The proscenium-style staging of the climactic event of the passion play understandably did not give any appropriate space to stage the gambling over the clothing of the savior during the scene of the dead Christ itself, and so the casting of dice was moved forward to the time just after Fr. Assenmacher's narrative sermon, and most if not all of the other dramatic activity directly associated with Christ's hours on the cross was lost.

Mr. Otero's text tells what comes next—"Joseph and Nicodemus take the body down from the cross, and Nicodemus takes him in his arms and gives him to his most holy mother. They wrap him in a winding sheet" (p. 3). This is the same ceremonial that is still performed in the Albuquerque parish of San Felipe each Good Friday. As the faithful enter San Felipe Church, they are confronted by a lifesize bulto of Christ on a tall cross in front of a large black drape that conceals the sanctuary and the altar. After the recitation of the first twelve stations, the priest preaches a sermon in the form of a prayer to Christ dead on the Cross. Then eight men, whose positions have passed down from father to son through the years, reenact the Thirteenth Station by removing the statue. Seven of the men steady cross, bulto, and ladder and the eighth ascends at the back of the cross. He removes the crown of thorns and the nails from the hands, passes a long white cloth between the hinged arms of the bulto and the arms of the cross and across the chest, and holding the two loose ends behind the ladder, he lowers the statue into the arms of the other men, who place it carefully into an open coffin somewhat like the one at Tomé. Two black-clad women who serve as official parish mourners and whose positions, like those of the men, descend from mother to daughter, help to arrange it. Then the casket is borne from the church on the shoulders of the eight men in a candlelight procession around Old Town Square, accompanied by the entire congregation singing hymns, and returned to the head of the main aisle for the remainder of the Thirteenth Station, the Fourteenth, and the concluding ceremonial, during which the members of the congregation file forward to reverence the five wounds of Christ by kissing them.

Unfortunately, the Tomé movie does not show the deposition at all, but resumes instead with the emergence of Christ's coffin from the church borne on the shoulders of six men and preceded by three small girls dressed in white who carry the implements of the passion, hammer, nails, and crown of thorns. With them are the black-clad Veronica and an "angelito" who holds "a napkin on which lie a few thorns," as Dr. Ellis will tell us shortly. In the movie, the bultos of Saint John and of Nuestra Señora de los Dolores appear in the background. Mr. Otero resumes:

> He [Christ] is embalmed and placed in the coffin, and carried to the Holy Sepulchre. The lining of the coffin is silk, the coffin is covered with fresh flowers. After he is placed in the coffin, the people put perfume on him. During this procession, five stops are made to symbolize the five wounds of our Lord.

13

The centurion, at this time, also wears mourning (p. 4.)[14] The centurion is in mourning because he has been converted by his recognition of Christ as God's own Son (Mark 16:39); the purple dress of Christ's mocked kingship is now replaced on the centurion's spear by a black dress of mourning. The movie shows Fr. Assenmacher incensing the lattice-work casket as it rests on a table in the churchyard exactly as a real coffin is incensed after a Catholic requiem Mass.

Dr. Ellis gives a fuller account and interpretation of the procession that follows, which is shown only rather briefly in the film:

> And now the procession forms rapidly, led by the centurion dressed in black, with a black hood and handkerchief masking his face. This horseman carries the tall spear with an envelope containing the written conviction of Christ at its tip. Directly beneath is a black, doll-size dress, the garb of Christ now that He is dead, say the people. Earlier in the day the tiny dress had been purple, the color of kings.

> Behind the centurion is one of the churchmen, carrying the ten-foot black cross from within the church, the purple cloth draped from it. And following the cross, with the benign gravity of scrubbed angels, are three five-year-old girls wearing long white robes, their hair in neat ringlets. The two on the outside carry plates, one holding a modern hammer and very long nails, representing those which pierced the hands and feet of Christ, and the other a crown of savage thorns (p. 210).

Next come Veronica and the coffin, carried on the shoulders of six of the "Jews."

> Behind these men of dignity is a choir of women carrying the books from which they repeat the simple lament *Miserere Mei Deus,* and somewhere near is the player of the old *pito,* still giving forth a bird-like warble entirely unrelated to the melody of the lament.

> Following the choir four women carry an ancient three-foot wooden *bulto* of *Dolores,* Mother of Sorrows, dressed in black silk. A group of men follow with an equally old *bulto* of San Juan Nepomuceno, one of New Mexico's favorite saints, wearing a cassock of white filet from the hands of some ardent parishioner (p. 211).

I would like to take minor and redundant exception to Dr. Ellis' identification of the two bultos. The first-named of them I suggest is Mary under the title of Our Lady of Solitude; the Landavazo account is clear on this point. The mother of Christ, according to Spanish piety, retired from the world after the death of her son (and after his resurrection as well) and took up the life of a nun, and hence she is shown in a nun-like garb, ususally black with some white linen. And

14

the Saint John is certainly meant to be *taken* as the Evangelist, not John Nepomucene. Although the iconography of the statue in the movie points unquestionably to this latter saint—who is indeed "one of New Mexico's favorite saints," being the patron both of irrigation (he was martyred by drowning) and of Penitente secrecy (he was killed for refusing to reveal to a jealous king the contents of the queen's confession)—he had no connection as did the Evangelist with the passion and death of Christ. Dr. Ellis clearly points this out in her "Santeros of Tomé," a later article.[15] Indeed, the same bulto which represented Juan Nepomuceno most of the year and Juan Evangelista during the passion play served as Juan Bautista on that saint's feast day, June 24; finally, in 1953, Edwin Berry made a statue of Juan Evangelista which may still be seen in the Tomé museum.

> This, then, is the procession, except for the long lines of women (and a few men) which enclose singers and actors, and trail for a block behind them. If they move too slowly or too quickly, they are directed by the young Roman soldiers, whose red kilts and knee-laced sandals are but a background to the silver gleam of carefully imitated metal armor, and the crested helmets which some devout welder had cleverly cut and fashioned out of headgear salvaged from some war surplus shop. They carry spears, emblems of authority, but their speech is gentle—Spanish to the natives, English to the few Anglo visitors. Five times the procession halts and the heavy coffin is rested upon a table hastily brought to go beneath it, while the priest, who walks at its right side, incenses it. This is the procession of the Sainted Body, and when the plaza has been circled the coffin is carried in to the front of the church and placed at the altar rail, where all who wish may go to kneel beside it and have their medals touched to the sacred image by the three elderly apostles.
>
> This is the climax; the people kneel and file out slowly in little clusters (p. 211).

And Mr. Otero corroborates Dr. Ellis on this last recollection by noting that "it has been a very ancient custom for the people of the congregation to stay for some time outside the church, greeting one another and discussing the problems of the community" (p. 4).

Dr. Ellis says, in concluding her narrative, "There is a mass for Friday evening and the procession of *Nuestra Señora de la Soledád*; another mass for Saturday, and another for Sunday. But the play is ended" (pp. 211-12). Indeed, though, the play was not ended, according to the filmed version and the Landavazo-Berry-Zamora scenario. The ceremonies surrounding the Soledád sermon on Friday evening are simple enough; those of Saturday make only a slight addition to those of the Catholic Church as performed in every parish, perhaps because in Tomé Holy Saturday is the traditional—almost obligatory—day for planting chili.

Then on Easter Sunday morning, according to Mr. Otero,

> singing "Alleluia," the men file out of the church and make
> one group on the plaza, carrying the Redeemer who has
> arisen from the dead, and in another group walk the women
> with his most holy mother. Saint John, elated with joy, runs
> to carry the news to Mary most holy of the resurrection of
> her son. With the same joy he runs back and forth (between
> the other two statues as they approach one another). The
> meeting between Jesus and Mary most holy, his mother,
> moves the heart of every Christian. For ourselves, this is the
> most important moment in the whole drama, for it gives
> proof that Jesus Christ and his teachings have triumphed in
> the end. With a harmonious sound, the church bells
> announce the resurrection of the Redeemer of the world
> (p. 4).

The movie shows this scene very powerfully. The bulto of Christ which
took part in the Way of the Cross now has its new Easter head, is clad
in brilliant white, and holds in its right hand a staff with the banner of
Pascal victory. The statue of Saint John is borne on a pallet by two
men who literally do run back and forth between the two converging
statues of Christ and his mother, in a folk-theater interpretation of John
20:1-10. In the Landavazo account,

> Saint John goes running and meets Jesus Christ, embraces
> him, runs to where Mary most holy is approaching,
> embraces her, runs the other way to where Christ is coming
> and then the other way to where the Virgin is coming and
> continues so until Jesus Christ and the Virgin meet. They
> embrace and the procession continues.

The two main bultos, those of Christ and Mary, have again
encountered one another, and the same poignant spectacle which was
the sorrowful fourth station of the Way of the Cross on Friday is
transformed into the joyous restoration of the risen son to his mother.
After the symbolic salutation, the groups arrange themselves with those
carrying Christ followed by the children in front, the statues of Mary
and Saint John next, and the banners of the confraternities, priest,
sacristans, and choir bringing up the rear; and they return to the
church as the church bell joyfully announces to the countryside the
good news that Christ has risen from the dead.

The very conclusion of Dr. Ellis' fine article may serve us as an
ideal jumping-off point for assessing the deeper meanings of the Tomé
passion play. She writes, "The people have recalled their sins in seeing
Christ die for them. They have done penance by re-enacting the great
sin. They are penitent. They are descendants of the Penitentes" (p.
212).

These sentences may well give the impression—as indeed my own
second paragraph may even more strongly—that only the ceremonies
at Tomé and the rituals of the Penitentes can be validly compared; and
they were, as has been pointed out, for an interval closely intermixed
together. But it must be recalled that in New Mexico there was a

strong and longstanding tradition of religious folk drama apart from the passion plays and the rituals of the Penitente brotherhoods, a tradition which Dr. Ellis herself had carefully noted in the opening paragraphs of her article, and which Sister Joseph Marie has detailed in a lengthy monograph. Despite the scanty documentation of older New Mexican history, the titles and many of the texts of fifteen plays of some substance have come down to us: from the Old Testament, *Adán y Eva* and *Cain y Abel;* from the New, *Coloquio de San José, Las Posadas, Los Pastores, Los Reyes Magos, La Primera Persecutión de Jesús,* and *El Niño Perdido* (in addition, of course, to the passion play); from the history and legends of Spain, *Los Moros y los Cristianos* and *La Vuelta de Cruzado;* from that of Mexico, *La Aparición de Nuestra Señora de Guadalupe* and *Los Matachines;* and from that of New Mexico, *Los Padres, Los Comanches,* and *Los Tejanos.*[16] Whatever else is true, it must always be borne in mind that both penance and religious folk drama antedated both the New Mexican Penitentes and the Tomé passion play, and that the passion play must look for its closest cognates first of all to other drama.

These other dramas were, without exception, at least flavored with Catholicism; and this fact should come as no surprise, for they had developed from simple plays used to instruct the unlettered people of Old and New Mexico in the essentials of the Catholic faith. This faith was to a degree that can scarcely be overemphasized sacramental in character; it was centered around baptism, the Mass and the Eucharist, and confession, and also included devotions similar to the sacraments proper—the rosary, the way of the cross, elaborate wakes, various novenas and other prayers to favorite saints, and of course the santos—the religious statues and paintings of which Spanish Catholicism demanded a great number so that religion could be practiced as the people thought it should. Toward the end of the eighteenth century, with the rise of the Masonic movement throughout Europe, religious orders were either suppressed (the Jesuits) or progressively curtailed in their operations (the Franciscans). The hierarchy of the diocese of Durango moved to replace the friars in New Mexico with secular clergy but with altogether too few priests to accomplish the task satisfactorily; and when the new Mexican Republic ordered the expulsion of all Spanish-born clerics, New Mexico was left with fewer priests than ever before—and there had never been really enough friars to serve the large number of small settlements and to cover the immense breadth of territory the colony encompassed.

Under these circumstances, the devout laity of the area began more and more to substitute their own ceremonies for the absent ministrations of the clergy. Baptism, of course, they could themselves perform, and they could read the prayers for the dying and conduct funeral services; there were even provisions for contracting valid marriages when it might be foreseen that no priest would be available for a lengthy period of time, though the difficulty of dispensing

impediments of consanguinity became a problem.[17] But the very core of Catholic sacramentalism, the Mass and the Eucharist, were not to be performed by the laity, nor was confession—the sacrament of Penance.

It is my hypothesis, therefore, that deprived of the non-dramatic ritualization of the passion and death of Christ which Catholic theology has always held the Mass to be, the people of New Mexico responded by summoning up the priesthood of each Christian people and creating the various "folk sacraments" constituted by dramatizing in a ritual manner that very passion and death of Christ that are the dynamic center of Christianity. The earliest of these stratagems, so far as the available documents seem to indicate, was the Tomé passion play and any other similar ritual—for instance the one recorded in Santa Fe by W.W.H. Davis, in which a good Friday procession

> was preceded by a man mounted on a horse, intended to represent a centurion, who was surrounded by a Roman guard armed with spears, forming as villainous-looking a group as I had seen for a long time. The horse was led by two grooms, dressed in the same garb as the guard, who, to make him prance and show off in good style, pricked him constantly with short goads. Then came the dead body of Christ in an open coffin, on which were a number of small wooden images, with the usual accompaniment of saints and priests, and, while they marched, a choir of boys sang sacred music. The exercises closed with service in the church, and a torchlight procession in the evening.[18]

Now since Santa Fe would always have had a resident priest, it would be unreasonable to suggest that the only motivation for performing passion plays in New Mexico was supplying ceremonies in the absence of the clergy; but however much the people may have enjoyed engaging in the staging of their dramas, there was certainly a deep religious motivation operating, and not merely the love of theater and acting. From the point of view of the nineteenth-century priests, we may suspect that they saw in the Tomé and Santa Fe ceremonies a good way to undercut the drawing power of the Penitentes; from the point of view of the people, the enactments gave a concreteness to the passion and death of Christ which the Mass, because its ritualization of Calvary was so comparatively undramatic, tended to lack.

The Way of the Cross was available as a hint of the direction that seems to have been taken up both in the case of the santos and in the case of the Mass, with the stasis of the earliest santos and the rituality of the Mass converted through the dynamism of the Jesús Nazareno bultos into the dramatization of the passion plays and the Penitente ceremonials. In either of these dramatic representations, the people of the village could feel that by reenacting the death of Christ they have drawn as close as possible to the great redemption and have appropriated its benefits most efficaciously into the life of their village.

In 1955, the Tomé passion play was performed for the last time.

For the services of the next year, the Catholic Church introduced a new Holy Week liturgy, doing away with the old Tenebrae services and entirely altering the traditional time schedule. Further, there was greater difficulty (as Dr. Ellis has noted) in recruiting younger men and women to fill the places of those who had become feeble or died. And so the Passion Play ceased.

But some of the laity of the parish, acting very much in the spirit of their eighteenth-century forebears in Tomé, sponsored and led the Stations of the Cross on the Cerro de Tomé, a conspicuous volcanic hill in the environs of the town. The rite consisted only of recitation of the prayers and hymn-singing (led by a drum) as the procession wended its way up to the three very large crosses which crowned the summit of the 375-foot hill. Reports of the ceremonies speak of a frustrated plan to enact the part of Simon of Cyrene at the Fifth Station; and a pair of movies showing the ceremonies in two different years, taken by Mr. Ralph C. Castillo of Belén, show the leader of the Stations and the hymns, Mr. Edwin Berry, enacting Pontius Pilate's washing his hands at the First Station after reading the sentence of death. Unfortunately, even this simple substitute lasted for only a few years, and by about 1963 Tomé was left with nothing to distinguish it from the many other devout Spanish towns of New Mexico, nothing except the memories of a unique pageant which reached back into the eighteenth century and had annually made the lifegiving death and resurrection of Jesus Christ a vital, breathing presence in the village of Tomé.

FOOTNOTES

1 Josiah Gregg, Commerce of the Prairies in Reuben Gold Thwaites, ed. Early Western Travels (Cleveland: Arthur H. Clark, 1905), 20:48.

2 Fray Francisco Atanasio Dominguez, The Missions of New Mexico, 1776, transl., annot. by Eleanor B. Adams and Fray Angélico Chavez (Albuquerque: University of New Mexico Press, 1956), p. 154; Florence Hawley Ellis, "Passion Play in New Mexico," New Mexico Quarterly 22 (1952), 200-12. Page numbers for further references to this article by Dr. Ellis will be cited in the text.

3 Thomas J. Steele, S.J., Santos and Saints: Essays and Handbook (Albuquerque: Calvin Horn, 1974), pp. 45-71. Mary Austin, The Land of Journeys' Ending (New York: Century, 1924), p. 364, notes a ritual of the Talpa Penitentes in which an effigy was substituted for the Cristo, a man formerly chosen by the brotherhood; other penances continued to be practiced. Robert Adams, The Architecture and Art of Early Hispanic Colorado (Boulder: Colorado Associated University Press, 1974), p. 22, notes that "some plazas staged a cycle of plays during Holy Week that depicted the whole story of the capture, trial, and crucifixion of Christ."

4 F. Stanley, The Tomé, New Mexico Story (Pep, Texas: F. Stanley, 1966), pp. 3-9, 16; Frederick Webb Hodge and Charles Fletcher Lummis, eds., The Memorial of Fray Alonso de Benavidez: 1630, transl. Mrs. Edward E. Ayer (Albuquerque: Horn and Wallace, 1965 [orig. 1916]), p. 222.

5 Fray Angélico Chavez, "The Penitentes of New Mexico," New Mexico Historical Review 29 (1954), 108-12; Fray Angélico Chavez, My Penitente Land (Albuquerque: University of New Mexico Press, 1974), pp. 218-22; Gregg, pp. 48-49; the first man was surely acting in imitation of Christ, not of Simon of Cyrene.

6 Steele, pp. 171-73.

7 The gospel in question is John 18: 1-8, the beginning of the gospel appointed for Friday of Holy Week. The dialogue which follows is a folk version.

8 Judas is shown in the movie dressed as the other Jews are, except that his beard is black rather than white. Informants state that in former years the dubious privilege of playing this part passed down in one family from father to son, but that in recent years it rotated from person to person on a volunteer basis. See William E. Barrett's Shape of Illusion (Garden City: Doubleday, 1972), for a fictional account of the Judas role in a passion play, "second only to Jesus."

9 Florence Hawley Ellis, "Santeros of Tomé," New Mexico Quarterly 24 (1954), 353; Florence Hawley Ellis, "Tomé and Father J.B.R.," New Mexico Historical Review 30 (1955), 198-99, 219. The newer statue of Christ has interchangeable heads, one for the passion, the other for Easter.

10 G. Cyprian Alston, "Way of the Cross," The Catholic Encyclopedia (New York: Robert Appleton, 1912), 15:569-71; Bonaventure A. Brown, "Way of the Cross," New Catholic Encyclopedia (New York: McGraw-Hill, 1967), 14:832-35; Dominguez, p. 153. The ten older oil paintings presently in the Tomé church seem to date from the eighteenth century and hence would not have been described as "old" by Fray Benavidez. None of them would have been stations of the cross.

11 Ben M. Otero, "Semana Santa en Tomé," typescript, p. 2; my translation. Page numbers for further references will be given in the text.

12 Ellis, "Tomé and Father J.B.R.," p. 218.

13 Ellis, "Santeros of Tomé," pp. 349-50; Ellis, "Tome and Father J.B.R.," pp. 199-200.

14 Ellis, "Tomé and Father J.B.R.," p. 218, notes that the American flag on the pole atop the Memorial Monument was lowered to half-staff in mourning for the dead Christ.

15 Steele, pp. 178-79, 187-88. The bulto of Saint John the Evangelist presently at Tomé dates only from 1953; see Ellis, "Santeros of Tomé," p. 353; Ellis, "Tomé and Father J.B.R.," p. 199; the other statue seems to have been John Nepomucene for three hundred and sixty days of the year, John the Evangelist only during the passion play, and sometimes John the Baptist on June 24.

16 Ellis, "Passion Play in New Mexico," p. 201, names most of these plays; for the whole list, see Sister Joseph Marie McCrossan, The Role of the Church and the Folk in the Development of Early Drama in New Mexico (Philadelphia: University of Pennsylvania Press, 1948), pp. 1-5, 88-89, 95, 101-03. It should also be noted in this context that there has flourished a vital and widespread New Mexico Spanish tradition of folk balladry reaching down to the very present; see Richard Gardner, ¡Grito! Reies Tijerina and the New Mexico Land Grant War of 1967 (New York: Bobbs-Merrill, 1970), pp. 267, 281.

17 Pedro Bautista Pino in H. Bailey Carroll and J. Villasana Haggard, transl., eds., Three New Mexico Chronicles (Albuquerque: The Quivira Society, 1942), pp. 50-51.

18 W.W.H. Davis, El Gringo: or New Mexico and Her People (New York: Harper and Brothers, 1857), p. 346. The Holy Thursday procession was centered on the crucifix, and as the quotation indicated, the Good Friday ceremony on the dead body of Christ. This would seem to point to the control of the timing by the Divine Office of the priests, in which formerly the morning prayers of Holy Thursday, Matins and Lauds, were "anticipated" on Wednesday afternoon, those of Friday on Thursday, and those of Saturday on Friday; similarly the first celebration of the resurrection came on Saturday morning. See Herbert Thurston, Lent and Holy Week (London: Longmans, Green, 1904), pp. 238-73. The last eight pages of Thurston's chapter, incidentally, describe the official liturgical version of the "considerable noise" which the Penitente Tinieblas enlarged upon so effectively.

HOLY WEEK IN TOMÉ
A NEW MEXICO PASSION PLAY

HOLY WEEK IN TOME
ACCORDING TO THE SOCIETY OF SAINT JOSEPH

COMMISSION:
FRED LANDAVAZO
EDWIN BERRY
JUAN ESTEVAN ZAMORA

ILLUSTRATED
BY
FRED LANDAVAZO
TOME, NEW MEXICO
1947

(TRANSLATED BY
T.J. STEELE, S.J.)

SEMANA SANTA EN TOME
POR LA SOCIEDAD DE SAN JOSE

COMISION
FRED LANDAVAZO
EDWIN BERRY
JUAN ESTEVAN ZAMORA

ILUSTRADO
POR
FRED LANDAVAZO
TOME, NUEVO MEXICO
1947

TRADITIONAL CEREMONIES

THE CHURCH OF THE IMMACULATE CONCEPTION
OF TOME

APRIL 17, 1946.

Mr. Estevan Torrez — Director

Assistants
Rev. José Assenmacher
Mrs. Toribio Chavez
Mrs. Luís Baca
The Altar Society
The Society of the Sacred Heart
The Society of Saint Joseph.

DEPOSITO

IGLESIA DE LA INMACULADA CONCEPCION
DE TOME

ABRIL 17, 1946.

Sr. Estevan Torrez — Director

Asistentes
Rev. José Assenmacher
Sra. Toribio Chavez
Sra. Luís Baca
La Sociedad Del Altar
La Sociedad Del Sagrado Corazón
La Sociedad De San José.

DEDICATION

We dedicate this booklet with affectionate gratitude to all those persons who year after year have kept this religious tradition alive. To all those persons who up to the present have exerted themselves to preserve these beautiful and meritorious functions. To all those persons who have taken part in the various characterizations; and finally to every good Catholic who strives to spend Holy Week in Tomé.

DEDICATORIA

Dedicamos esta obra con afectuosa gratitud a todas aquellas personas quienes ano tras ano han revivido esta costumbre religiosa. A todas aquellas personas quienes aun ahora se esmeran para preservar estas hermosos y efectivos oficios. A todas aquellas personas quienes toman parte en las diversas representaciones, y por fin a todo buen catolico quien se esmera a pasar Semana Santa en Tomé.

PREFACE

For many years there has been a standing custom in the parish of Tomé. Traditionally, in years past, the people represented many more of the scenes of the passion of Our Lord Jesus Christ than those we now see here during Holy Week. It is quite remarkable that there has been nothing in writing about the procedures of these ceremonies, but that they have been passed from generation to generation, notwithstanding some changes, until finally they have come down to us such as we see them today.

It is the purpose of the Society of Saint Joseph in Tomé to preserve these customs, both for their spiritual value and for the moving religious atmosphere brought about by these ceremonies, sermons, and other activities so in keeping with our belief.

For the first time we attempt to put this very effective work on paper, with the sole desire that in the future we may continue to perform these representations and devotions with more polish, developing them more and more.

We ask God that we may be successful, and that our intentions may be sincere.

This ceremonial is divided into five acts. Each act corresponds to one day, beginning on Wednesday of Holy Week and ending on Easter Sunday. Moreover, each act is divided into scenes according to the services held each day. For instance, Good Friday has four different services, each making up one scene.

The actors are the statues of the holy persons of old, the people who carry them, and the people who take part in the various duties and representations, such as the priest, the servers, the Jews, the centurion, Judas, Pontius Pilate, and so forth, as well as those who act as ushers to preserve good order.

Here it should be noted that the actors are not the same throughout all the scenes, except that those who carry the statues are persons who by their very nature are prone to be helpful, either urged by some vow or just for the pleasure of being of help. Only when there are not enough persons volunteering their services does the director nominate others from those who are already present.

PREFACIO

Por muchos anos se ha acostumbrado deposito en la parroquia de Tomé. Se cuenta que en anos pasados aun se representaban muchas mas de las escenas de la pasion de Nuestro Senor Jesucristo que las que ahora vemos durante Semana Santa. Lo mas curioso es que no se encuentra nada escrito acerca del procedimiento de estos ejercicios, sino que se han ido pasando de generacion a generacion, no obstante con algunos cambios, hasta por fin llegar a nosotros tal como ahora los vemos.

Es el proposito de la Sociedad de San Jose de Tome preservar estas contumbres, tanto por su valor espiritual como por el ambiente religioso y pinturesco causados por estos ejercicios, sermones y oficios tan armoniosos con nuestra creencia.

Por primera vez no esforsamos a darle escritura a esta tan efectiva obra con el solo deseo que en lo futuro sigamos llevando estas representaciones y devociones con mas esmero desarrollandolas mas y mas.

Quiera Dios que tengamos buen excito, que nuestras intenciones son sinceras.

Esta obra esta dividida en cinco actos. Cada acto representa un dia. Principiando el Miercoles Santo y terminando el Domingo de Resurrecion. En cambio cade acto esta dividido en escenas a sugun de servicios hay cada dia. Por ejemplo el Viernes Santo hay cuatro diferentes oficios, cada oficio representa una escena.

Los personajes son las estatuas de los santos antiguos, las personas quienes las llevan, y las personas quienes toman parte en los oficios y representaciones, como son el sacerdote, los sacristanes, los judios, el centurion, Judas, Poncio Pilato etc, tanto como los que derigen y guardan el buen orden.

Aqui se debe de notar que los personajes no son los mismos para todas las escenas sino que los que llevan las estatuas son gente que a ellos mismas les ha nacido ayudar, ya sea por alguna promesa o por el gusto de servir. Solo cuando no hay suficiente gente ofreciendo su servicio el derictor nombra a otros de entre los que estan presentes.

As has been said above, it is our hope to preserve as well as to develop and augment these ceremonies, and for this purpose some space will be left at the bottom of each page for giving further explanations which might clarify and increase the interest of what has been described or illustrated, and for adding from time to time other notes which may be more helpful.

Further, the better to explain and give a more exact notion to the reader of the various scenes and characters and their locations, as well as to make the booklet more interesting, some simple illustrations have been included.

In concluding these preliminary remarks, we wish to express our gratitude for their contributions and explanations to the Rev. Fr. José Assenmacher, Don Julian Zamora, Don Estevan Torrez, the ladies of the Altar Society, and all those who have offered their aid in bringing about the completion of this booklet.

The commission—Fred Landavazo
Edwin Berry
Juan Estevan Zamora

Como se a dicho desde en antes, es el proposito de preservar tanto como desarrollar y engrandecer estas contumbres y por eso al pie de cada pagina se ha reservado un espacio para dar explicaciones que puedan aclarar y dar mas interes a lo que se ha escrito o se esta representando y para anadir de vez en cuando otras notas que sean para mas provecho.

Tambien para mejor explicar y para dar una idea al lector de las diferentes escenas, los personajes y sus posiciones tanto como para hacer este libro mas interesante, se han incluido algunas simple illustraciones.

Para terminar deseamos expresar nuestra gratitud por sus contribuciones y explicaciones al Rev. Padre Jose Assenmacher, a Don Julian Zamora, a Don Estevan Torrez, a las Senoras de la Sociedad del Altar, y a todos aquellos quienes ofrecieron sus servicios para que esta obra se llevara acabo.

La comision—Fred Landavazo
Edwin Berry
Juan Estevan Zamora.

IGLESIA CATOLICA, TOME, N. MEX..

WEDNESDAY OF HOLY WEEK   APRIL 17, 1946

PERSONAGES

The Priest ....Rev. Fr. José Assenmacher

The Servers ....Hermenes Sanchez, Tony Sanchez,
Meliton Sanchez, Doroteo Baca

The Blood of Christ[1] ....carried by Fred Landavazo

The Choir ....

Two men to direct the procession ....Mr. Juan Estevan Zamora
Mr. Elauterio Sanchez

A man to act as usher
for the people ....Mr. Manuel A. Baca

The people ....All who are in attendance and
take part in the processions.

---

1 This is the crucifix hanging to the south of the sanctuary in the Tomé church. Florence Hawley Ellis, "Santeros of Tomé," New Mexico Quarterly 24 (1954), 347-48, assigns it to Antonio Silva and dates it about 1795.

Miss Esquipula Zamora was for many years in charge of the upkeep of the santos and their costumes.

MIERCOLES SANTO   ABRIL 17, 1946

PERSONAJES

El Sacerdote ....Rev. Padre Jose Assenmacher

Los Sacristanes ....Hermenes Sanchez, Tony Sanchez,
Meliton Sanchez, Doroteo Baca

La Sangre De Cristo ....Llevada por Fred Landavazo

El Coro ....

Dos hombres para derigir la procesion ..Sr. Juan Estevan Zamora
Sr. Elauterio Sanchez

Un hombre para acomodar
a la gente ....Sr. Manuel A. Baca

La gente ....Todos los que atienden y
forman las procesiones.

WEDNESDAY OF HOLY WEEK

TENEBRAE[2]

ACT ONE

The action takes place within the church at the main altar and later during the procession through the plaza.

It begins at seven in the evening.

In front of the main altar there are two candelabra with fifteen lighted candles on each.

The priest and the servers enter. The priest prays the office of Tenebrae. The candles are put out one after the other until all have been extinguished. At that time the servers make noise with the matracas.[3] When this has been done the procession of the Most Precious Blood moves through the plaza. There are two lines of persons walking one by one led by two servers who carry lanterns made of red glass, followed by the boys and girls of the school and by the women and the men.

In the middle walk the priest, the servers, the Blood of Christ, and the choir. They sing "Miserere Mei Deus."

---

2 Tenebrae, a portion of the divine office (the breviary) comprising Matins and Lauds for Holy Thursday, was "anticipated" on Wednesday evening. The Tinieblas ceremonies, developed by the Penitentes into quite a memorable service, is developed from it; in Tomé it would have been comparatively restrained.

3 Matracas are ratchet noisemakers of wood.

"MISERERE MEI, DEUS"[4]

PSALM 50

Have mercy on me, O God, according to thy great mercy.

And according to the multitude of they tender mercies blot out my iniquity.

Wash me yet more from my iniquity, and cleanse me from my sin.

MIERCOLES SANTO

LAS TINIEBLAS

ACTO PRIMERO

El escenario toma lugar adentro de la iglesia en el altar mayor y despues la procesion por la plaza.

Tiempo a las 7:00 de la tarde.

En el frente del altar major hay dos candeleros con quince velas encendidas en cada uno.

Entran el socerdote y los sacristanes. El sacerdote resa los oficios de las Tinieblas. Las velas se van apagando una tras otra hasta que se han apagado todas. Entonces los sacristanes sueran las matracas. Terminados estos oficios sale la Procesion de la Preciosisima Sangre por la plaza. Se hacen dos filas de a uno guiadas por dos sacristanes los cuales llevan faroles con luces rojas. Siguen los ninos y las ninas de la escuela, las mujeres y los hombres.

Enmedio van el Sacerdote, los sacristanes, La Sangre De Cristo y el coro. Se canta "Miserere Mei Deus."

"MISERERE MEI, DEUS"

PSALMUS L

Miserere mei, Deus, secundum magnam misericordiam tuam;
Et secundum multitudinem miserationum tuarum, dele
    iniquitatem meam.
Amplius lava me ab iniquitate mea,
Et a peccato meo munda me.

For I know my iniquity, and my sin is always before me.

To thee only have I sinned, and have done evil before thee: that thou mayst be justified in thy words, and mayst overcome when thou art judged.

For behold I was conceived in iniquities; and in sins did my mother conceive me.

For behold thou hast loved truth: the uncertain and hidden things of thy wisdom thou hast made manifest to me.

Thou shalt sprinkle me with hyssop, and I shall be cleansed: thou shalt wash me, and I shall be made whiter than snow.

To my hearing thou shalt give joy and gladness: and the bones that have been humbled shall rejoice.

Turn away thy face from my sins, and blot out all my iniquities.

Create a clean heart in me, O God: and renew a right spirit within my bowels.

Cast me not away from thy face; and take not the holy spirit from me.

Restore unto me the joy of thy salvation, and strengthen me with a perfect spirit.

I will teach the unjust thy ways: and the wicked shall be converted to thee.

Deliver me from blood, O God, thou God of my salvation: and my tongue shall extol thy justice.

O Lord, thou wilt open my lips: and my mouth shall declare thy praise.

For if thou hadst desired sacrifice, I would indeed have given it: with burnt offerings thou wilt not be delighted.

A sacrifice to God is an afflicted spirit: a contrite and humbled heart, O God, thou wilt not despise.

Deal favourably, O Lord, in thy good will with Sion; that the walls of Jerusalem may be built up.

Then shalt thou accept the sacrifice of justice, oblations and whole burnt offerings: then shall they lay calves upon thy altar.

---

4 The Douay-Rheims English is presented here as probably the nearest equivalent to the Spanish Catholic understanding of this psalm in nineteenth-century New Mexico.

Quoniam iniquitatem meam ego cognosco,
Et peccatum meum contra me est semper.
   Tibi soli peccavi, et malum coram te feci;
Ut iustificeris in sermonibus tuis,
Et vincas cum iudicaris.

   Ecce enim in iniquitatibus conceptus sum,
Et in peccatis concepit me mater mea.
   Ecce enim veritatem dilexisti;
Incerta et occulta sapientiae tuae manifestasti mihi.
   Asperges me hyssopo, et mundabor;
Lavabis me, et super nivem dealbabor.
   Auditui meo dabis gaudium et laetitiam,
Et exsultabunt ossa humiliata.
   Averte faciem tuam a peccatis meis,
Et omnes iniquitates meas dele.

   Cor mundum crea in me, Deus,
Et spiritum rectum innova in visceribus meis.
   Ne proiicias me a facie tua,
Et spiritum sanctum tuum ne auferas a me.
   Redde mihi laetitiam salutaris tui,
Et spiritu principali confirma me.
   Docebo iniquos vias tuas,
Et impii ad te convertentur.
   Libera me de sanguinibus, Deus, Deus salutis meae,
Et exsultabit lingua mea iustitiam tuam.

   Domine, labia mea aperies,
Et os meum annuntiabit laudem tuam.
   Quoniam si voluisses sacrificum, dedissem utique;
Holocaustis non delectaberis.
   Sacrificium Deo spiritus contribulatus;
Cor contritum et humiliatum, Deus, non despicies.
   Benigne fac, Domine, in bona voluntate tua Sion,
Ut aedificentur muri Jerusalem.
   Tunc acceptabis sacrificium justitiae, oblationes et holocausta;
Tunc imponent super altare tuum vitulos.

When they arrive back at the front of the church, the people line up on either side until the priest, the servers, the Most Precious Blood of Christ, and the choir have passed into the church. Then all the people enter. When all have come in, the priest gives them his blessing.

Notes and explanations: There is also singing during the Tenebrae office.

First the procession.

HOLY THURSDAY   APRIL 18, 1946

ACT TWO
SCENE ONE

The mass is at eight. After the mass the Most Holy Sacrament is carried to the altar of repose in the small chapel.[5] The Ladies of the Altar Society and the Society of the Sacred Heart accompany it. Then they make visits and keep vigil all day beginning about 8:30 and lasting until six in the evening.

Notes and explanations: They sing "Vuestro Cuerpo Sacrosanto"; the people respond.

---

5 The chapel of repose is the enclosed room to the north of the sanctuary. —Informants ·state that "Pues Padeciste, Tan Desolda" and "A Jesus Yo Quiero Acudir" were also sung at this time. The choir also sang the Latin hymn "Pange Lingua."

Al llegar de vuelta al frente de la iglesia la gente se afila a un lado y otro hasta que pasan el sacerdote, los sacristanes, La Preciosisima Sangre De Cristo y el coro. Despues entra toda la gente. Cuando todos han entrado el sacerdote echa la bendicion.

Notas y explicaciones: Tambien se canta durante los oficios Tenebre.
Primero la Procesion.

JUEVES SANTO   ABRIL 18, 1946

ACTO SEGUNDO
ESCENA PRIMERA

La misa a las ocho. Despues de la misa se deposita el Santisimo Sacramento del Altar en la capillita. Las Senoras de la Sociedad del Altar y la Sociedad del Sagrado Corazon lo acompanan. Despues se hacen visitas y se vela todo el dia empesando mas o menos a las ocho y media hasta 6:00 pm.

Notas y explicaciones: Se canta—"Vuestro Cuerpo Sacrosanto;" La gente responde.

"VUESTRO CUERPO SACROSANTO"

Let your Most Holy Body
Be my sweet companion,
Which to eternal rest
Conducts me without fear.

Your Most Holy Body
Is sustenance for the weak,
Is food for the strong,
Is holiness for the sinner.

Your Most Holy Body
Is the life of my soul,
Health, sweet repose
Which mitigates my sorrow.

Your Most Holy Body
Is perfume so delightful;
It offers the nard of Carmel
And the lilies of Tabor.

Your Most Holy Body
Is most gentle rest
Where the soul in prison
Fully enjoys her lover.

Your Most Holy Body
Bears wounds, five nests,
Five chosen shelters,
Which are fuel for its love.

Let your Most Holy Body,
O Jesus of my soul,
Feed me in my hour of death
That I may die in your love.

VUESTRO CUERPO SACROSANTO

Vuestro Cuerpo Sacrosanto
Sea mi dulce compañero
Que al descanso duradero
Me conduzca sin temor.

Vuestro Cuerpo Sacrosanto
Es de débiles sustento
Es de fuertes alimento
Es el bien del pecador

Vuestro Cuerpo Sacrosanto
Es la vida de mi alma,
La salud, la dulce calma,
Que mitiga mi dolor.

Vuestro Cuerpo Sacrosanto
Es fragancia, y más consuelo;
Da el nardo del Carmelo
Y los lirios del Tabor.

Vuestro Cuerpo Sacrosanto
Es suavisima morada,
Donde el alma aprisionada
Goza libre a su amador.

Vuestro Cuerpo Sacrosanto
Llagas tiene o cinco nidos,
Cinco albergues escogidos,
Que son pábulo a su ardor.

Vestro Cuerpo Sacrosanto
¡Oh Jesús del alma mía!
Sea manjar en mi agonía,
Con que espire en vuestro amor.

"PUES PADECISTE, TAN DESOLDA"

**Since you suffered
In such desolation,
Be propitious to us,
Blessed Mary.**

Now from the tomb
Sadly withdraws
The affectionate Mother,
So distressed.

On Calvary
She lies prostrate;
There they return,
All her sorrows.

She turns her eyes
And raising them on high
Adores the cross,
The beloved cross.

She follows the way
And the bloody tracks
She encounters, her Son's
Holy footsteps.

Soon to the retreat
Of her dwelling,
And there begins
The new anguish.

On her bloved Son
Sadly she reflects,
His cruel tragedy
Which torments her soul.

Her meditation
On his pain and anguish
Sorrowful reflections
Presented to her.

PUES PADECISTE, TAN DESOLDA

**Pues padeciste
Tan desolada,
Sednos propicia,
María sagrada.**

Ya del sepulcro
Triste se aparta
La tierna Madre:
¡Qué acongojada!

En el Calvario
Yace postrada;
Allí renueva
Todas sus ansias.

Los ojos vuelve,
Y enarbolada
La cruz adora
Enamorada.

Sigue el camino,
Y ensangrentadas
De su Hijo encuentra
Las huellas santas.

Luego al retiro
De su morada,
Y allí comienza
Nueva batalla.

De su amante Hijo
Triste repasa,
La cruel tragedia
Que angustia su alma.

Su pensamiento
De penas y ansias
Tristes objetos
Le presentaba.

Praying to the Father,
Him she contemplated
In the garden,
His soul in anguish.

Bloodthirsty wolves
She imagined,
Who would her Lamb
Take prisoner.

By a fierce man
Buffeted cruelly,
His beautiful face
You see so mistreated.

In a harsh prison,
Queen of Heaven,
The Son of God
Your heart adores.

Harsh Herod - -
A white tunic
As on a foolish man
You see placed on him.

At a pillar
They were scourging him,
And in that torment
Your soul meditates on him.

With sharp thorns
They crowned him;
His royal forehead
You contemplated.

You listen to the "Ecce Homo"
Pronounced
By the judge; and the people
Cry, "Let him die!"

That he die in shame
You hear the command
Of the President,
And he has decreed it.

Orando al Padre
Le contemplaba
En aquel huerto
Su alma angustiada.

Sangrientos lobos
Se figuraba
Que a su Cordero
Preso llevaban.

De un hombre fiero
Cruel bofetada
Su rostro bello
Ve que maltrata.

En dura cárcel,
Reina Sagrada,
De Dios el Hijo
Adora tu alma.

Herodes terco
Túnica blanca
Como a hombre necio,
Ves le aplicaba.

A una columna
Le flagelaban,
Y en aquel tormento
Le atiende tu alma.

De agudos juncos
Que coronaban
Sus reales sienes
Considerabas.

"Ecce Homo" escuchas
Que pronunciaba
El juez; y el pueblo,
¡Que muera!, clama.

Que muera infame
Oyes que manda
El Presidente,
Y esto firmaba.

The heavy tree
Which oppressed him,
You see how to the earth
It prostrates him.

Your poignant encounter
You relive,
When on the way to Calvary
He journeyed along.

Arriving at the mountain
You see them mistreat him,
And when they have nailed him
They embitter him with gall.

The cruel nails
Transfix your soul,
And the hammers
Have echoed in your heart.

And still you watch him
When they raise him
Upon the cross,
Surrounded by taunting men.

Forsaken
He calls—you hear him—
To the eternal Father
With a bitter complaint.

And as he is in agony
Thirst torments him
With greater suffering
So that he pants in his suffering.

That he has completed
Our souls'
Redemption
He says in a loud voice.

El duro leño
Que le agobiaba
Por tierra veías
Que le postraba.

Tu encuentro tierno
Le renovabas,
Cuando al Calvario
Se encaminaba.

Llegando al monte
Ves le maltratan,
Y ya clavado
Con hiel le amargan.

Los crueles clavos
Tu alma traspasan,
Y los martillos
Te resonaban.

Ya le contemplas
Que le levantan
En el madero
Entre algazara.

Desamparado
Oyes que clama
Al Padre Eterno
Con queja amarga.

Ya agonizante
La sed le abrasa
De más tormentos
Que anhela y ansia.

Que ha consumado
De nuestras almas
La Redención,
Dice en voz clara.

And into the holy hands
Of the Father, his soul
You see him entrust
And die in his anguish.

From that gibbet
They lower the dead one,
And in your lap
You contemplate his body.

But your pain
And your anguish
Now increase
When you no longer have him.

Between your sobs
You lament,
Finding yourself alone—
O bitter pain!

Such a little dove,
Abandoned,
Without husband or son
You bemoan your bereavement.

Alas, loving Mother,
So desolate!
Only pain
Accompanies you.

Lift up your eyes,
Holy Queen,
To those of your son
Which cry for your notice.

Y en santas manos
Del Padre su alma
Ves que encomienda,
Y espira entre ansias.

De aquel cadalso
Muerto le bajan,
Y en tu regazo
Le contemplabas.

Pero tus penas,
Pero tus ansias
Aquí se aumentan
Cuando no le hallas.

Entre sollozos
Te lamentabas
Viéndote sola;
¡Oh pena amarga!

Cual tortolilla
Desamparada
Viuda y sin Hijo
Gimes tus ansias.

Ay, tierna Madre,
¡Que desolada!
Sólo las penas
Os acompañan.

Tus ojos vuelve,
Reina Sagrada
A esos tus hijos,
Que a ellos claman.

"A JESUS YO QUIERO ACUDIR"

To Jesus I wish to go,
Jesus I desire to see,
Jesus I wish to obey,
Jesus forever to serve. Amen.

Good Jesus, listen to me today,
Good Jesus, take pity on me,
Good Jesus, help me;
Good Jesus, o pardon me!

With Jesus, my heart is at rest,
With Jesus is its security,
With Jesus it will be pure
With Jesus, it can achieve anything.

Of Jesus I shall always speak,
By Jesus I am always helped,
By Jesus I am loved,
With Jesus I am and will remain.

In Jesus I always find pity,
In Jesus I find repose,
In Jesus I find my joy,
In Jesus my felicity.

Jesus was always patient,
Jesus was most benevolent,
Jesus was sweet, was loveable,
Jesus was always forgiving.

Great is Jesus, always great,
Great is my Jesus in wisdom,
Great is my Jesus in Power,
Jesus is great, my all in all.

Make me, Jesus, patient,
Make me, Jesus, loving;
Make me, Jesus, faithful,
Make me, Jesus, patient.

A JESUS YO QUIERO ACUDIR

A Jesús yo quiero acudir,
A Jesús yo deseo ver,
A Jesús quiero obedecer,
A Jesús por siempre servir. Amén.

Buen Jesús, hoy escúchame,
Buen Jesús, compadéceme,
Buen Jesús, favoréceme;
Buen Jesús, ¡ah! perdóname.

Con Jesús, mi alma descansa
Con Jesús está segura,
Con Jesús será muy pura,
Con Jesús todo se alcanza.

De Jesús yo siempre hablaré,
De Jesús siempre ayudado,
De Jesús enamorado,
De Jesús soy y seré.

En Jesús siempre hallo piedad,
En Jesús hallo reposo,
En Jesús encuentro gozo,
En Jesús mi felicidad.

Fué Jesús siempre paciente,
Fué Jesús el más afable,
Fué Jesús dulce, fué amable,
Fué Jesús siempre clemente.

Grande es Jesús, siempre grande
Grande es mi Jesús en saber,
Grande es mi Jesús en poder,
Grande es Jesús y mi todo.

Hacedme, Jesús, sufrido,
Hacedme, Jesús, amante:
Hacedme, Jesús, constante,
Hacedme, Jesús sufrido.

Jesus is our Redeemer,
Jesus, all my consolation,
Jesus, my own pure longing,
Jesus the magnet of my love.

Light of Jesus, vital light,
Light of Jesus which creates anew,
Light of Jesus, might I see you,
Light of Jesus, might I live in you.

My Jesus, may you be praised,
My Jesus, be you blessed,
My Jesus, let me love you,
My Jesus, let me adore you.

Never can Jesus deceive me,
Never does Jesus wish to afflict me,
Never does Jesus fail to hear me,
Never does Jesus wish to fail me.

O Jesus, infinite in love,
O Jesus, gentle Lamb,
O Jesus, true God;
O my Jesus, my Savior.

For Jesus my ardent zeal,
For Jesus I wish to live,
For Jesus I wish to die,
For Jesus alone.

Who will not surrender himself to Jesus?
Who is not in debt to Jesus?
Who can refuse love to Jesus?
Who would not submit to Jesus?

Jesus is king by his very being,
Jesus is king, the King of kings,
Jesus is king and gives commands,
Jesus is king of clemency.

Be thou, my Jesus, my protector,
Jesus, be my light and guide,
Jesus of my soul, be,
Be, my Jesus, my protection.

Jesús es nuestro Redentor,
Jesús, todo mi consuelo,
Jesús, blanco de mi anhelo,
Jesús el imán de mi amor.

Luz de Jesús, luz activa,
Luz de Jesús, que recrea,
Luz de Jesús, que te vea,
Luz de Jesús, yo en ti viva.

Mi Jesús, sed alabado,
Mi Jesús, sed bendecido,
Mi Jesús, sed mi querido,
Mi Jesús, sed mi adorado.

Ni Jesús puede engañarme,
Ni Jesús quiere afligirme,
Ni Jesús deja de oírme,
Ni Jesús quiere dejarme.

Oh Jesús, infinito amor,
Oh Jesús, manso Cordero,
Oh Jesús, Dios verdadero;
Oh mi Jesús, mi Salvador.

Por Jesús mi celo ardiente,
Para Jesús quiero vivir,
Para Jesús quiero morir,
Para Jesús únicamente.

¿Quién a Jesús no se entrega?
¿Quién a Jesús no es deudor?
¿Quién a Jesús niega el amor?
¿Quién a Jesús no sosiega?

Rey es Jesús, por esencia,
Rey es Jesús, Rey de reyes,
Rey es Jesús, que da leyes,
Rey es Jesús, de clemencia.

Sed, mi Jesús, mi protector,
Sed, Jesús, mi luz y guía,
Sed Jesús del alma mía,
Sed, mi Jesús, mi defensa.

I have in Jesus cure for ill,
I have in Jesus total safety,
I have in Jesus pure holiness,
I have in Jesus light divine.

Come, Jesus, we pray you,
Come, Jesus, to protect us,
Come, Jesus, to help me,
Come, Jesus, O come soon.

I, my Jesus, am fatigued here,
Jesus, I thank you a thousand times,
Jesus, I am always yours,
I, my Jesus, with a new life.

Zeal for Jesus, take hold of me,
Zeal for Jesus, convert me,
Zeal for Jesus, direct my steps,
Zeal for Jesus, take hold of me.

Blessed be my Jesus
In the heavens and on the earth;
And blessed be as well
His most beloved Mother. Amen.

Tengo en Jesús medicina,
Tengo en Jesús cabal salud,
Tengo en Jesús pura virtud,
Tengo en Jesús luz divina.

Venid, Jesús, os lo ruego,
Venid, Jesús, a ampararnos,
Venid, Jesús, a ayudarme,
Venid, Jesús, venid luego.

Yo, Jesús, aquí rendido
Yo, Jesús, mil gracias os doy,
Yo, Jesús, siempre vuestro soy,
Yo, Jesús, con nueva vida.

Zelo de Jesús, prendedme,
Zelo de Jesús, habladme,
Zelo de Jesús, guiadme,
Zelo de Jesús, tenedme.

Bendito sea mi Jesús
En los cielos y en la tierra;
Y bendita sea también
Su muy querida Madre. Amén.

HOLY THURSDAY   APRIL 18, 1946

SCENE TWO

PERSONAGES

The Priest ....Rev. Fr. José Assenmacher.

The Servers ....Doroteo Baca, Olmedo Baca,
David Sanchez, Tony Sanchez,
Meliton Sanchez, Hermenes Sanchez

The Divine Presence ....carried by Miguel M. Salazar,
Fred Landavazo, Rumaldo Garcia,
Francisco Baca

The Most Holy Virgin ....carried by Mrs. Meliton Torrez,
Mrs. Juan Estevan Zamora, Mrs. Fred Landavazo,
Mrs. Frank D. Baca

The Holy Cross ....carried by Crestino Baca

Saint John ......carried by Seferino Sanchez, Nicanor Sanchez

An angel who carries the chalice ....Mary Lou Baca

The centurion (mounted on horseback) ....Ramón Chavira

The Roman soldiers ....Hermenes Baca, Jimmy Otero,
Antonio J. Baca, Julian Torrez,
Elizar Torrez, Louie Padilla,
Robert Sanchez

Judas Iscariot ....(wrapped in a white
cloak and carrying a hangman's
noose in his hand) — Prudencio Marquez

The Jews (carrying staff) ....Bennie Marquez, Elias Chavira,
Jesús Baca, Eugenio Sanchez,
Antonio Chavira, Tony Perea,
Juan Barela, José Rafael Sanchez,
Castulo Zamora (he plays the flute)

The choir ....The same as in the first act

JUEVES SANTO   ABRIL 18, 1946

ESCENA SEGUNDA

PERSONAJES

El Sacerdote ....Rev. Padre Jose Assenmacher.

Los Sacristanes ....Doroteo Baca, Olmedo Baca,
David Sanchez, Tony Sanchez,
Meliton Sanchez, Hermenes Sanchez

El Divino Rostro ....Llevado por Miguel M. Salazar,
Fred Landavazo, Rumaldo Garcia,
Francisco Baca

La Santisima Virgen ....Lleveda por Sra. Meliton Torrez,
Sra. Juan Estevan Zamora, Sra. Fred Landavazo,
Sra. Frank D. Baca

La Santa Cruz ....Llevada por Crestino Baca

San Juan ......Llevado por Seferino Sanchez, Nicanor Sanchez

Un Angel que lleva el caliz ....Mary Lou Baca

El Centurion (montado acaballo) ....Ramon Chavira

Los Solados Romanos ....Hermenes Baca, Jimmy Otero,
Antonio J. Baca, Julian Torrez,
Elizar Torrez, Louie Padilla,
Robert Sanchez

Judas Escariote (envuelto en una sabana blanca
y lleva la soga en la mano.) ....Prudencio Marquez

Los Judios (llevan lanzas) ......Bennie Marquez, Elias Chavira,
Jesus Baca, Eugenio Sanchez,
Antonio Chavira, Tony Perea,
Juan Barela, Jose Rafael Sanchez,
Castulo Zamora (toca el pito)

El Coro ....Los mismos del primer acto

LOS SOLDADOS ROMANOS Y LOS JUDIOS   TOME 8/11/47

JESUCRISTO ES PRENDIDO

HOLY THURSDAY   APRIL 18, 1946

SCENE TWO

The action takes place within the church at the main altar and later during the procession through the plaza.

It begins at three in the afternoon.

In the sanctuary of the church is the Divine Image.[6]

The choir sings "Agonisante en el Huerto" before the sermon.

---

6 This is the Jesús Nazareno statue used to represent Christ except during the crucifixion and burial.

"AGONISANTE EN EL HUERTO"

In his agony in the Garden
We now consider the Lord
Pressing his face to the earth
In a sweat of blood.

**O Jesus, for my sins
You suffered such sorrow;
At your feet, repenting,
Look at me, sweet Redeemer.**

In the pretorium we see him
Scourged with great fury;
Covered with chain-blows is
The Lord, for mankind.

With insults and torture
The brutal mob wreathes
A spiked crown
On the forehead of the Lord.

The meek lamb they load
With the cross of sorrow;
His heavy load to the hills
The sweet Savior carries.

JUEVES SANTO   ABRIL 18, 1946

ESCENA SEGUNDA

El escenario toma lugar adentro de la iglesia en el altar major y despues la procesion por la plaza.
Tiempo a las 3:00 de la tarde.
En el frente esta El Divino Rostro.
Antes del sermon se canta "Agonisante en el Huerto."

AGONIZANTE EN EL HUERTO

Agonizante en el huerto
Contemplamos al Señor,
Postrado en tierra su rostro
Con un sangriento sudor.

On Jesús, por mis delitos
Padeciste tal dolor:
A tus pies arrepentido
Me ves, dulce Redentor.

En el pretorio le vemos
Azotado con furor:
Es de cadenas cubierto
Por los hombres el Señor.

Con las afrentas y dolores
Ciñe la tropa feroz
Una punzante corona
En la frente de su Dios.

Al cordero manso cargan
Con el leño del dolor;
Su pesada cruz a cuestas,
Marcha el dulce Salvador.

Jesus nailed to the cross
Contemplate, O sinner;
Look at the Son of the Eternal
Dying for love of you.

*   *   *

The priest and sacristans enter.
The priest preaches the sermon on the capture of Christ.

A SERMON ON THE CAPTURE OF CHRIST
BY THE REVEREND FATHER JOSE ASSENMACHER
THREE IN THE AFTERNOON—HOLY THURSDAY

In the name of the Father and of the Son and of the Holy Spirit, amen.

I HAVE GIVEN YOU AN EXAMPLE.

It is with a heavy heart that we must meditate upon the holy death of our Savior. The unique event in the history of the world is the passion of our Redeemer, which is depicted in the traditions and customs of so many different places.

The church also teaches us during Holy Week to meditate on the passion. There is beauty here and there is sadness. This morning we had to contemplate the Last Supper of Holy Thursday, a day not only of sorrow but also one of beauty, commemorating the Most Holy Sacrament. Jesus Christ took bread, blessed it, broke it, gave it to his disciples, and said, "Take, and eat: this is my body." And taking the chalice, he gave thanks and gave it to them, saying, "Drink of this all of you, for this is my blood. I am the pathway of truth, and of eternal life."

I HAVE GIVEN YOU AN EXAMPLE.

And to climax his last farewell, before he went forth, he enobled all people. Beneath the appearances of the bread he gave us the life of the spirit and a guarantee of life eternal.

With the Most Holy Sacrament in the Holy Mass, we commemorate his passion. "This is my body, this is my blood." With vibrant faith let us adore our Lord become the Sacrament, and let us go forward toward a death undergone to ensure life, consolation and fortitude to prevail in this vale of tears.

A Jesús en cruz clavado
Contémplace, oh pecador;
Ve al Hijo del Eterno
Expirando por tu amor.

* * *

Entra el socerdote y los sacristanes.
El sacerdote da el Sermon del Prendimiento.

SERMON DEL PRENDIMIENTO
POR EL REVERENDO PADRE JOSE ASSENMACHER
TIEMPO—A LAS 3.00 DE LA TARDE DEL JUEVES SANTO

En el nombre del Padre y del Hijo y del Espiritu Santo amen.

EJEMPLO OS HE DADO.

Bajo este moto debemos meditar la santa muerte de nuestro Salvador. El hecho unico de la historia universal es la pasión de nuestro Redentor que fue illustrada en tantas diversas veces en tradiciones y costumbres.

La iglesia también nos enseña en Semana Santa meditar en la pasión. Hay hermosura y hay dolor. Esta mañana hemos meditado sobre la ultima cena del Jueves Santo, no solo un día de tristeza sino también de consolación, comemorando el Santisimo Sacramento. Jesucristo tomó el pan, lo bendició, lo partió y se lo dió a sus dicipulos, y dijo, "Tomad, y comed: este es mí cuerpo." Y tomando el Caliz, dió gracias y se los dió deciendo: "Bebed de este todos porqué esta es mi sangre. Yo soy el camino de la verdad, y de la vida eterna."

OS HE DADO EJEMPLO.

Y para coronar su ultima despedida, antes de salir corono toda la gente. Bajo el pan dió vida sublime y garantia a vida eterna.

Bajo el Santisimo Sacramento en la Santa Misa comeramos su pasión. "Este es mi cuerpo, esta es mi sangre." Con viva fe hemos adorado a nuestro Senor Sacramentado y vamos hasta morir para tener vida, consolación y fortaleza para vencer este valle de lagrimas.

Thursday is a holy day of sorrow and yet also a day of glory and consolation. All the gospels narrate the Last Supper. Here the final commandment is given; here the Apostles say, "We will follow you," but Jesus replies, "This chalice you cannot drink. Here the new commandment: charity, love of one another; and for this I offer my body under the appearances of bread. Love one another as I have loved you; do not strike blow for blow, do not knock out tooth for tooth.

"I have given you an example, that you love each other."

If this had been realized two thousand years ago this would not be a vale of tears. Where do all the crimes and wars originate? From pardoning as Christ pardoned? From giving example as he did, up to the end of his life?

It is hard to understand, since Jesus was not merely a man but was God himself. In this regard, year after year we have considered various themes of the passion of Our Lord. One time we meditate on the theme, "Follow Jesus Christ"; another time, "The Five Wounds"; last year we contemplated "The Holy Places"; and today, somewhat similarly, "I Have Given You an Example."

Live as He lived and not as we desire. All the world is nothing in comparison with the passion of Our Lord. Wonder at Our Lord washing his disciples' feet, giving us example.

"I have come not to be served but to serve." But mankind has always been opposed to this, ever since Adam and Eve. If they did not hold themselves opposed to the commandment of God we would not behold any such thing as the passion of our Lord.

Peter sensed and knew that Jesus was more than a mere man and objected, saying, "You will not wash my feet." Jesus said to him, "You will be nothing that belongs to me; if I do not wash your feet, you will not attain salvation." Then Peter responded, "Then wash my head and all of me."

Another friend, Judas—who would have done much better to have followed these examples—had sold Christ the day before for a mere thirty pieces of silver. Falling into despair, he hanged himself from a tree upon realizing his treachery.

Jesus Christ with the other eleven proceeded to the Mount of Olives and he said to them, "Remain here while I go a little ways on and pray." There he began to sweat blood, in a terrible agony, for he saw and knew all that he would suffer. He saw Judas, he saw Peter, he saw Pontius Pilate, he saw his Way of the Cross and all that would happen. When he would be lifted up onto the cross: what awful torment. He felt the blows, the

Jueves Santo dia de tristesa tambien dia de gloria y consolacion. Todos los evangelios comenzaron con la ultima cena. Aquí un ultimo mandado, y los Apostoles dijeron, "Tu ejemplo vamos a seguir," pero Jesus les dijo, "No pueden tomar este Caliz. Aquí un nuevo mandado. Caridad, amarse uno al otro y por eso ofresco mi cuerpo en especie de pan. Amarse el uno al otro como yo os he amado, no dar golpe por golpe y diente por diente.

"Ejemplo yo os he dado que se amen."

Si esto ubiera sido realizado dos mil anos despúes este no fuera un valle de lagrimas. De donde vienen todas las bromas y guerras? Van a perdonar como yo he perdonado? Van a dar ejemplo hasta que acaben con su vida?

Deficil es comprender, porqué Jesus no fue solo un hombre sino Dios mismo. Por eso, año por año hemos meditado diversos temas de la pasion de Nuestro Senor. Una vez meditamos sobre el tema: "Seguir a Jesucristo." Otra vez, "Las Cinco Llagas," El año pasado meditamos sobre, "Los Lugares Santos," Y hoy algo semegante, "Ejemplo Os He Dado."

Vivir como El vivió y no como deseamos. Todo es nada en comparación de la pasion de Nuestro Senor. Mirad a Nuestro Senor lavando los pies de sus dicipulos, dando ejemplo.

"Vine, no para ser servido sino para servir." Pero el hombre siempre ha sido opuesto desde Adan y Eva. Si ellos no se ubieran opuesto al mandado de Dios no tuvieramos la pasión de nuestro Senor.

Pedro sintio y sabia que Jesus era mas que hombre y se opuso diciendo, "No me laves los pies." Jesus le dijo, "No es eso lo que hago, si no te lavo los pies no alcanzaras la salvacion." Entonces Pedro respondió, "Pues lavame la cabeza y lavame todo."

Otro amigo, Judas que podía muy bien haber seguido estos ejemplos, el dia antes lo vendió por solo trienta monedas de plata. Desesperado se fue para un arbol para realizar su enfieldad.

Jesucristo con los otros once se fué al Monte De Los Olivas y dijo a su dicipulos, "Sentaos aqui mientras voy alli y hago oracion." Alli estuvo sudando sangre, fue una agonia terrible, porque vió y supo todo lo que iba a padecer. Vió a Judas, vió a Pedro, vió a Poncio Pilato, vió su Via Crucés y todo lo que ocurrió. Como fué elevado en la cruz, terrible tormento. Sintió golpes, burlas, insultos escupiendole el rostro, sintió espinas y

jests, the insults spit at his face, the crown of thorns, and he saw his Mother. It was a terrible being he saw upon that cross covered with red pearls, shedding fervent tears for those who would turn traitor. Thus he began sweating blood and praying for Jerusalem.

The moon gave her light and he saw Jerusalem, Jerusalem which would not be converted despite so many miracles. Nevertheless, he has not yet died, he who wished to convert it. He has asked its soul and it has refused.

Jesus sought consolation. His mother was not with him. His friends were asleep, and so he asked Peter, "Did you not have the strength to watch only one hour with me?" Turning, he moved away and in his anguish of agony and bloody sweat asked for consolation from his heavenly Father. "Father in heaven, can this chalice pass without my having to drink it?"

"You have wished it; if you wish it no more, there can be no redemption for the human race. It is not my will but your will."

Jesus replied, "Whatever your will chooses I am ready for."

The mob came like thieves in the night to capture Our Lord, and with them came Judas, whom Jesus could easily have destroyed except that he preferred to die himself.

And so in the same way we go to follow the Holy Scripture and imitate the good example of Our Lord Jesus Christ.

In the name of the Father and of the Son and of the Holy Spirit, amen.

The angel offers Christ the chalice.

After the sermon the priest reads the gospel of Good Friday,[7] breaking off where Judas betrays Our Lord:

—At that time Jesus went forth with his disciples over the brook Cedron, where there was a garden, into which he entered with his disciples. And Judas also, who betrayed him, knew the place; because Jesus had often resorted thither together with his disciples. Judas therefore having received a band of soldiers and servants from the chief

---

7 For the angel offering Christ the chalice, see three citations in the synoptics, Mt. 26:39; Mk. 14:36; Lk. 22:42; the gospel of Good Friday is John 18 and 19, the passion narrative. The Jews, of course, do not use the title "King of the Jews."

vió a su Madre. Una cosa terrible se vió en la cruz cubierto de perlas coloradas, sudando fervorosas lagrimas por aquellos que fueron traidores. Asi estubo sudando y rezando por Jerusalen.

La luna dió y vió a Jerusalen, Jerusalen que no quizo convertirse apesar de tantos milagros. Obstante no ha muerto quién quizo convertirle. Le a pedido el alma y el alma no ha querido.

Jesus buscaba consolación. Su madre no estubo con El. Sus amigos durmiendo, y por eso le dice a Pedro, "Conque no habeis podido velar ní una sola hora conmigo?" Volvió alejarse y en sus ancias de agonia sudando sangre buscó consolacion en su padre celestial. "Padre Celestial, puedes pasar este caliz sin que yo lo beba?"

"Tu has querido, si no quieres, no hay redencion por la humanidad. No es mi voluntad sino tu voluntad."

Jesus respondio, "Que se haga tu voluntad estoy listo."

Llegáron los canallas como ladrones en la noche para prender a Nuestro Senor, y con ellos uno, Judas, quién Nuestro Senor bien podia vengar, pero mejor quizo morir.

Asi tambien nosotros vamos a seguir la Sagrada Escritura y emitar los buenos ejemplos de Nuestro Senor Jesucristo.

El el nombre del Padre, y del Hijo, y del Espiritu Santo Amen.

El angel ofrece el caliz.

Terminado el sermon el sacerdote lee al Evangelio del Viernes Santo terminando donde Judas entrego a Nuestro Senor:

En aquel tiempo marcho Jesus con sus discipulos a la otra parte del torrente de Cedron, donde habia un huerto, en el cual entro con sus discipulos. Judas que lo entregaba, estaba bien informado del sitio; porque Jesus solia retirarse muchas veces a el con sus discipulos. Judas, pues, habiendo tomado una cohorte o compania de soldados y varios ministros que le dieron los pontifices y fariseos, fue

priests and the Pharisees, cometh thither with lanterns and torches and weapons. Jesus therefore, knowing all things that should come upon him, went forth.

Just then Judas enters, clothed in a white cloak and carrying a hangman's noose in his hand. The Jews are following him.

THE PRIEST:—Whom seek ye?

THE JEWS.—Jesus of Nazareth, King of the Jews.

THE PRIEST.—(continuing to read the gospel)

Jesus saith to them: I am he. And Judas also, who betrayed him, stood with them. As soon therefore as he had said to them: I am he; they went backward, and fell to the ground. Again therefore he asked them (turning to ask): Whom seek ye?

THE JEWS.—Jesus of Nazareth, King of the Jews.

THE PRIEST.—(turning for a third time to ask)—Whom seek ye?

THE JEWS.—Jesus of Nazareth, King of the Jews.

THE PRIEST.—I am he; here I am.

Judas places the noose around the neck of the Divine Image and ties his hands [with the loose end]. When this is over, the procession sets forth, during which the choir sings "Pues Padeciste."

"PUES PADECISTE"

Since you suffered
For love of us,
Blessed Jesus,
Be my remedy.

Praying to the Father
You I see in the Garden,
Your holy blood
Watering the earth.

Bloodthirsty wolves
Capture him quickly,
And take him to Annas—
Christ the lamb.

alla con linternas, y hachas, y con armas. Y Jesus, que sabia todas las cosas que le habian de sobrevenir, salio a su encuentro.

Aqui entra Judas cubierto con una sabana blanca y lleva la soga en la mano. Los Judios le siguen.

EL SACERDOTE.—A quien buscais?

LOS JUDIOS.—A Jesus Nazareno Rey de los Judios.

EL SACERDOTE.—(sigue leeyendo el Evangelio)

Diceles Jesus: Yo soy. Estaba tambien entre ellos Judas el que lo entregaba. Apenas, pues, les dijo: Yo soy, retrocedieron todos, y cayeron en tierra. Levantados que fueron, les pregunto Jesus segunda vez (vuelve el sacerdote a decir): A quien buscais?

LOS JUDIOS.—A Jesus Nazareno Rey de los Judios.

EL SACERDOTE.—(vuelve por tercera vez a preguntar)—A quien buscais?

LOS JUDIOS.—A Jesus Nazareno Rey de los Judios.

EL SACERDOTE.—Yo soy y aqui estoy.

Judas le pone la soga al Divino Rostro en el cuello y le ata las manos. Terminado este oficio sale la procesion; en la procesion se canta "Pues Padeciste."

PUES PADECISTE

**Pues padeciste
Por amor nuestro,
Jesús bendito,
Sed mi remedio.**

Orando al Padre
Te veo en el huerto,
Tu sacra sangre
Regando el suelo.

Sangrientos lobos
Le llevan preso
Y a Anás presentan
Aquel cordero.

A cruel beating
Some fierce man gives,
Thereby offending
That beautiful countenance.

In a hard prison,
O God eternal,
You suffer humbly
The cruel torment.

A white garment
Harsh Herod
To his guest, Jesus;
How foolish a man.[8]

At a column
Hard tied,
Filled with wounds
His holy body.

From sharp thorns[9]
They have made a crown
And from a mean reed
They have made a scepter.

"Ecce homo," says
The leader to the people
But he only asks
He should die soon.

Pilate signs the decree[10]
Against my master
That he die in disgrace
Upon the tree.

8 Contrast this stanza with the thirteenth stanza of "Pues Paedciste, Tan Desolada."

9 The Spanish word juncos literally means "reeds." It would be tempting to see this as a reference to the use of yucca leaves by the Penitentes in their Holy Week services.

10 Beginning with this stanza, the hymn follows the Stations of the Cross with the exception of Station Ten—though there may be a stanza missing.

Cruel bofetada
Da un hombre fiero,
Con que lastima
Su rostro bello.

En dura cárcel
¡Ah! Dios eterno,
Sufres humilde
Crueles tormentos.

Túnica blanca
Herodes terco
A Jesús viste,
Cual hombre necio.

A una columna
Atado atiendo
Lleno de llagas
Su santo cuerpo.

De agudos juncos
Corona han hecho,
Y de vil caña
Le dan el cetro.

Ecce Homo, dice
El juez al pueblo,
Más éste pide
Que muera luego.

Pilatos firma
Contra mi dueño
Que muera infame
En un madero.

Already he takes up the cross,
My Nazarene—
O that my sins
Are that burden!

Three times defeats him
That heavy load,
Falling, the Son
Of the Father Eternal.

His beloved Mother
He tenderly meets,
And leaves wounded
The heart of them both.

The pious woman
Offers him a towel
And the holy countenance
Receives as reward.

Those who weep
For his sufferings
He tells to weep
For themselves and their children.[11]

With cruel nails
To the harsh tree
The executioners nail
All heaven's king.

From the cross
The Word has spoken,
Teaching the truth
To the universe.

11 *Since Stations Three, Seven, and Nine are grouped together three stanzas before, Stations Six and Eight come in two immediately adjacent stanzas. This may account for their apparent juxtaposition in the services as shown by the movie.*

Ya la cruz carga
Mi Nazareno,
¡Ay, que mis culpas
Son aquel peso!

Tres veces postra
El duro leño
En tierra al Hijo
Del Padre Eterno.

Su amable Madre
Encuentra tierno,
Y queda herido
De ambos el pecho.

Mujer piadosa
Le ofrece un lienzo,
Y el rostro santo
Recibe en premio.

A los que lloran
Por sus tormentos
Que lloren manda
Por si y por deudos.

Con crueles clavos
En tronco acerbo
Clavan verdugos
Al rey del cielo.

De la cruz hace
Cátedra el Verbo,
Dando doctrina
Al universo.

From the first
He prayed for those
Who tormented him,
Our priceless exemplar.[12]

Heaven he offered
To a thief, who straightforth
Acknowledged him
His supreme King.

Soon he entrusted,
Filled with love,
To Saint John his Mother
From that time on.

Abandoned
By the infinite God,
He complained sorrowfully
Of his great grief.

The sufferings follow
And already, in thirst,
He says he endured
The greatest pains.

When he is dying
He calls out the mystery
Of redemption,
Which was his purpose.

And into the holy hands
Of the Eternal Father
He delivers his spirit
And his final breath.

A soldier arrives
With a cruel lance,
And opens his breast,
That happy portal.

12 The seven stanzas beginning with this one give the "Seven Last Words" of Christ on the cross, all taken from scripture; see Luke 23:34; Luke 23:43; John 19:26-27; Matthew 27:46 and Mark 15:34; John 19:28; John 19:30; Luke 23:46.

En la primera
Ruega por éstos
Que le atormentan,
Con raro ejemplo.

La gloria ofrece
A un ladrón, recto
Ya en confesarlo
Su Rey supremo.

Luego encomienda,
De amores lleno
A Juan su Madre
Desde aquel tiempo.

Desamparado
De Dios inmenso,
Se queja triste
De sentimiento.

Siguen las penas,
Y ya sediento
Dice que se halla
De más tormentos.

Que está acabado,
Clama el misterio,
De redimirnos,
Que era su intento.

Y en santas manos
Del Padre Eterno
Entrega su alma
Y último aliento.

Llega el soldado,
Con cruel acero
Su costado abre
Que es feliz puerto.

From that gallows
And royal throne
They lower his body
Wholly destroyed.

His tender Mother
Prepares a bed
In her lap
To receive him.

And in the grave
Before unused—
In this coffer
They leave him closed.

Since so many sufferings
Are an echo of love,
Blessed Jesus,
Be my remedy.

ORDER OF THE PROCESSION

1. The Centurion goes ahead on horseback.
2. The Herald.
3. The Holy Cross.
4. The boys and girls of the school.
5. The women and the men.

IN THE MIDDLE

1. The angel with the chalice.
2. Judas.
3. The official.
4. The Divine Image.
5. The Most Holy Virgin.
6. Saint John.
7. The priest.
8. The servers—the soldiers.

De aquel cadalso
Y trono regio
Su cuerpo bajan
Todo deshecho.

La tierna Madre
Prepara lecho
En su regazo
Para su centro.

Y en un sepulcro
Del todo nuevo
Aquel santuario
Queda cubierto.

Pues penas tantas
Son de amor eco,
Jesús bendito,
Sed mi remedio.

ORDEN DE LA PROCESION

1. El Centurion va adelante montado acaballo.
2. El Pregonero.
3. La Santa Cruz.
4. Los ninos y ninas de la escuela.
5. Las mujeres y los hombres.

ENMEDIO

1. El angel con el caliz.
2. Judas.
3. El oficial.
4. El Divino Rostro.
5. La Santisima Virgen.
6. San Juan.
7. El sacerdote.
8. Los Sacristanes—los soldados.

9. The Choir—(singing "Pues Padeciste" [and] "La Pasion"[13]

On returning to the front of the church, they follow the same procedure as on Wednesday. The people stay in line, and wait there until all those who take active part in the scene have entered. As soon as all are within, the priest gives his blessing.

---

13 "La Pasion" is an alternate name for "Mi Dios y Mi Redentor."

"MI DIOS Y MI REDENTOR"

My God and my Redeemer,
In whom I hope and trust,
Through your passion, my Jesus,
Embrace me in your love.

Listen, be alert
To what Jesus suffered
From the garden to the cross
In his sacred passion;
Tears of devotion
May the Lord give each of us.

Afflicted and tormented
See him in his prayer,
And suffering his passion
He has sweated blood in the garden;
Down to the earth it has flowed
So copious his sweat.

They have dragged him in chains
And bound his arms;
Past the cruel bonds
The blood flows forth;
And they bear him off a prisoner
Like a man who has done wrong.

82

9. El Coro—(se canta "Pues Padeciste," "La Pasion")

Al llegar al frente de la Iglesia se sigue el mismo procedimiento que el Miercoles Santo. La gente se alinea, y aguardan hasta que entran todos los que toman parte en esta escena. Una vez todos adentro, el socerdote hecha la bendicion.

MI DIOS Y MI REDENTOR

Mi Dios y mi Redentor
En quien espero y confío,
Por tu pasión mío,
Abrasadme en vuestro amor.[14]

Escucha con atención
Lo que padeció Jesús,
Desde el huerto hasta la cruz
En su sagrada pasión:
Lágrimas de devoción
Nos dé a todos el Señor.

Afligido y angustiado
Lo verás en la oración,
Y sintiendo su pasión
Sangre en el huerto ha sudado;
Hasta la tierra ha llegado
Lo copioso del sudor.

En la prisión lo arrastraron,
Y a los brazos con cordeles
Echando lazos crueles
La sangre le reventaron;
Y así preso lo llevaron
Como a un hombre malhechor.

---

14 Only the third and fourth lines of this chorus are repeated after each stanza. Perhaps because of this the hymn is often known as "La Pasión."

With a hand armed with iron
On the innocent cheek
They strike a blow so brutal
That it makes the blood burst forth;
My God, that a stubborn heart
Should be the source of such harshness.

O, that someone had been there,
My sweet lover and master,
And the blow of each Jew
Had taken on his face for your sake!
All the guilt is mine alone
But you have suffered for it, Lord.

With rage and fury they lead him
From one tribunal to another,
And judge him with such bias
That they treat him like a fool;
And comparing him with Barabbas
They say Jesus is the worse.

He is stripped and scourged
With such terrible fierceness
That from head to foot
Is all one wound;
O how dearly he has paid
For his love of the sinner.

With piercing thorns
They crown his brow
And pressing them down hard
Transfix the divine forehead,
Opening thus the mines
Of something more precious than gold.

High on a balcony
Pilate pronounces "Ecce Homo";
And the ungrateful crowd,
"Let him die on the cross,"
So that even seeing him so wounded
Does not appease their hatred.

Con mano de hierro armada
A la mejilla inocente
Dan tan recia bofetada,
Que hacen que en sangre reviente,
Mi Dios, pues el alma siente
Ser causa de tal rigor.

¡Oh quién estuviera allí,
Dulce amante y dueño mío,
Y al golpe de aquel judío
Pusiera el rostro por tí!
Toda la culpa está en mí,
Y Vos la pagáis, Señor.

Con furia y rabia es llevado
De uno en otro tribunal,
Y lo miraron tan mal,
Que de loco lo han tratado;
Y con Barrabás mirado,
Dicen que Jesús es peor.

Desnudo está y azotado
Con tan terrible fiereza,
Que desde el pie a la cabeza,
Lo verás todo llagado;
¡Oh, qué caro le ha costado
El querer al pecador!

Con penetrantes espinas
Coronaron su cabeza,
Y apretándolas con fuerza
Rompen las sienes divinas,
Abriendo así las minas
Del oro de más valor.

En el balcón asomado,
"Ecce Homo" dice Pilato;
Y responde el pueblo ingrato
"Que muera crucificado"
Que aún con verlo tan llagado
No está saciado el rencor.

The obstinate people insist
On Jesus' death:
O my God, who would believe
That you would be condemned
To the death of the cross
Who are the author of life?

The crowd hears a lying herald
Who, to the sound of the trumpet
With all listening,
Says Christ is an imposter,
A sorcerer who must die
On the cross as a traitor.

Set upon and exhausted
And his beautiful cheeks
Filthy with spittle,
Insulted and made ugly,
Barefoot and all wounded
He walks, and to see him is sorrow.

With his heavy burden
And his crown of thorns
He walks bent over
Revealed as the Lamb;
Then a fierce executioner beats him
Brutally with a whip.

To encounter him has come
The mother who bore him.
And she sees him among the killers
Reviled and spit upon;
Her heart is cleft
By the sword of sorrow.

Again he has fallen, shoved
With brutal, inhuman fierceness,
And instead of helping him up
They prod him with goads
And with blows and derision
They make their Lord rise.

Insta el pueblo porfiado
Sobre que Jesús muriera:
O mi Dios ¿quién tal creyera,
Que tú fueses sentenciado
A morir crucificado,
Siendo de la vida autor?

Se oye el falso pregnonero,
Que al eco de la trompeta,
Y estando todos alerta,
Dice que es un embustero
Y que muera el hechicero
En una cruz por traidor.

Afligido, fatigado
Y la mejillas hermosas
Con salivas asquerosas,
Denegrido y afeado
Descalzo y todo llagado
Va, que el verlo es un dolor.

Con su pesado madero,
Y de espinas coronado,
El cuerpo lleva inclinado
El manifiesto Cordero;
También tira un sayón fiero
De la soga con furor.

Al encuentro le ha salido
La madre que le parió.
Y entre sayones le vió
Arrastrado y escupido;
Su corazón fué partido
Con espada de dolor.

Ya lo han caído a empellones
Con rigor fiero e inhumano,
Y en vez de darle la mano
Le dieron de puntillones,
Y con golpes e irrisiones
Levantan a su Señor.

A Cyrenian they have conscripted
To help carry the cross,
For they fear that Jesus
Will die before being crucified;
For this they have found help,
Not for pity or mercy.

He is covered with dust and sweat
When Veronica sees him,
And wiping the face of Christ
She finds it marked on the cloth;
Her care is bountifully rewarded
For he is generous paymaster.

He has come with the heavy cross
To Calvary, and quickly
They brutally strip off
His holy vesture;
The flesh is torn away, stuck
To the inner tunic.

Denuded and forced to his knees
In the sight of his Mother
He offers himself to the Father for you
Out of love for all men;
Gall and vinegar they have given him
To torment him the more.

And now stretched on the cross
See the cruel nail's
Point on his right hand
And the hammer poised;
O what a blow it has delivered
That it makes the Creator tremble.

His left arm they have tied down
With a noose of small cords,
And pulling it cruelly
They stretch out his frame;
New blows resound
As they hammer furiously.

Un Cireneo han hallado
Que ayude a llevar la cruz,
Porque temen que Jesús
Muera y no crucificado;
Por esto se lo han buscado:
No por piedad ni favor.

Lleno de polvo y sudado
La Verónica le ha visto,
Y limpiando el rostro a Cristo
En el lienzo fué estampado:
Bien se lo pagó el cuidado,
Porque es muy buen pagador.

Llegó con la cruz pesada
Al Calvario, y con presteza
Le quitaron con fiereza
La vestidura sagrada;
La carne salió pegada
A la túnica interior.

Desnudo y arrodillado,
Y a la vista de su Madre,
Se ofrece por ti a Dios Padre
En caridad abrazado:
Hiel y vinagre le han dado
Para tormento mayor.

En la cruz ya recostado
Verás de un clavo tirano
La punta en su diestra mano
Y un martillo levantado;
¡Oh, qué golpe ha descargado
Que hace temblar al Creador!

A la siniestra le echaron
Lazos con unos cordeles,
Y tirando muy crueles,
Los huesos le desencajaron;
Nuevos golpes resonaron
Al clavarle con furor.

Finally they fasten his legs
And pulling the frail body
They tug so as to stretch it
And wholly disjoint it;
They drill through the feet
The better to nail them.

Then after they have nailed him
As cruelly as they wish,
They turn the cross face down
And clinch the nails;
They stretch the wounds
Without pity or remorse.

Then they raise him on high
Blasphemed by his killers,
And between two robbers
Thirsting and forsaken
His body is broken
And blackened in color.

The sun has already hidden itself,
The earth continually trembling,
The temple veil tearing,
And the rocks make a noise;
The whole globe is afflicted
When the Savior dies.

An insolent soldier,
Seeing that Jesus has died,
With a spear has opened
His most holy side;
Water and blood have spilled out
For the benefit of the sinner.

Let it be, Sovereign Lord,
That by this wound of love
With divine ardor will burn
Every Christian heart,
And all the human race
Acknowledge you Redeemer.

También las piernas ataron
Y estando el cuerpo encogido
Tiran tanto que extendido
Todo lo descoyuntaron;
Los pies se los barrenaron
Para clavarlos mejor.

Después que así lo enclavaron,
Como tan mal le quisieron,
Boca abajo lo volvieron,
Y los clavos remacharon:
Las llagas las arrastraron
Sin piedad y sin temor.

En el alto está levantado,
Blasfemado de sayones
Y en medio de dos ladrones,
Sediento y desamparado,
Su cuerpo está destrozado,
Y denegrido el color.

El sol ya se ha obscurecido,
La tierra se ve temblando,
El velo se va rasgando,
Y las piedras hacen ruido;
El mundo está conmovido
Cuando muere el Salvador.

Un atrevido soldado,
Viendo que Jesús ha muerto,
Con una lanza le ha abierto
El santísimo costado:
Agua y sangre ha derramado
Para bien del pecador.

Haced, Señor Soberano,
Que en esa llaga de amor
Se abrase en divino ardor
Todo Corazón cristiano,
Y todo el género humano
Os confiese Redentor.

JESUCRISTO EN LA CARCEL

And let it be, my beloved Jesus,
That my eyes become fountains
Weeping burning tears
For how much I have sinned;
And since you have cost him so much
May you give generously in return.

HOLY THURSDAY   APRIL 18, 1946

SCENE THREE

PERSONAGES

The Priest ....Rev. Fr. José Assenmacher.

The Servers ....Doroteo Baca, Olmedo Baca,
David Sanchez, Tony Sanchez,
Meliton Sanchez, Hermenes Sanchez

Three little angels who carry the crown, the nails, the hammer, and a broom

They offer incense.

The Jews ....The same as in the afternoon.

Our Lord Jesus Christ ....(In prison with his hands tied
and the rope around his neck.
There are two candles on each
side of the prison.)

The choir ....The same as in act one.
Choir and people sing "Pues Padeciste por Amor Nuestro" (above).
The scene takes place within the church at the main altar.
The time is seven in the evening.
Enter—The three little angels.
They take their places in front of Our Lord Jesus Christ. Then they offer him incense.

94

Y haced, mi Jesús amado,
Que mis ojos hechos fuentes
Lloren lágrimas ardientes
De lo mucho que he pecado:
Y pues tanto os ha costado,
Y sois liberal dador.

JUEVES SANTO   ABRIL 18, 1946

ESCENA TERCERA

PERSONAJES

El Sacerdote ....Rev. Padre Jose Assenmacher.

Los Sacristanes ....Doroteo Baca, Olmedo Baca,
David Sanchez, Tony Sanchez,
Meliton Sanchez, Hermenes Sanchez

Tres Angelitos que llevan la corona los clavos el martillo y una escoba

---

Ofrecen insencio.

Los Judios ....Los mismos de la tarde.

Nuestro Senor Jesucristo ....(En la carcel con las manos atadas
y la soga en el cuello. Has dos
candeleros a cada lado de la carcel.)

El coro ....Los mismos del primer acto
    Coro y gente cantan "Pues Padeciste por Amor Nuestro"
(arriba).
    El escenario toma lugar adentro de la iglesia en el altar
mayor.
    Tiempo a las 7:00 de la tarde.
Entran—Los tres angelitos.
    Se sientan a delante de Nuestro Senor Jesucristo. Despues
ofrecen inciensio.

The Jews who keep watch over Our Lord.
The Servers.
The Priest.
The priest delivers a sermon on the captivity.

A SERMON ON THE CAPTIVITY OF CHRIST
BY THE REVEREND FATHER JOSE ASSENMACHER
SEVEN IN THE EVENING—HOLY THURSDAY

In the name of the Father and of the Son and of the Holy Spirit, amen.

My brothers in Christ, we continue to meditate on the passion of Our Lord under the theme "I Have Given You an Example."

Under the appearances of bread Our Lord has wished to live with us, to give us eternal life and fortitude, and to show us the way through life to eternity.

He was a servant who came to serve others and not to be served. The Son of the Omnipotent God, he still owned nothing in this world; even his manger was borrowed. The birds have their nests, the wolves their dens, but I, said this man, I have nothing.

I HAVE GIVEN YOU AN EXAMPLE.

He gave us an example by washing the feet of his disciples, and when he was in need of them they were sleeping. Watching alone, he sweated blood in his solitude for our sins. His disciples could not watch even an hour with him.. Our Lord was not obliged to undergo suffering; it was his free will to do so, out of love for his brethren. He handed over his human life to death for the sake of our salvation and eternal life.

So great was his power that, as Saint John has written, when the Jews came to seize him and he asked them, "Whom do you seek?", they replied, "Jesus of Nazareth," and he said, "I am he," they fell to the ground. Judas and the others knew who spoke, not a mere man but God himself. Cornelius also recognized him during the crucifixion.

Three times he said to them, "Whom do you seek?" Our Lord knew everything. Our Lord, who was all the heart could desire, was delivered over by Judas, who came like a serpent, traitor and hypocrite, pretending to be a friend; but Jesus knowing his intention asked, "Why have you come?"

Los Judios que velan a nuestro Senor.
Los sacristanes.
El Sacerdote.
El sacerdote da el sermon del Posentio.

SERMON DEL POSENTIO
POR EL REVERENDO PADRE JOSE ASSENMACHER
TIEMPO—JUEVES SANTO A LAS 7:00 DE LA NOCHE

En el nombre del Padre y del Hijo y del Espirito Santo amen.

Hermanos en Cristo. Hemos meditado la pasion de Nuestro Senor bajo el tema, *Ejemplo Os He Dado.*

Nuestro Senor bajo el especie de pan quizo vivir con nosotros, para darnos vida eterna, y fortaleza, para ensenarnos el camino de la vida y la eternidad.

El servidor que vino para servir pero no ser servido. Hijo de Dios Onipotente, no tenia nada en la vida, un pesebre fue prestado. Las aves tienen sus nidos, los lobos sus cuevas, yo, dijo el hombre no tengo nada.

EJEMPLO OS HE DADO.

Ejemplo nos dió lavando los pies de sus dicipulos, y cuando los necesitaba se durmieron. El solo velando en su soledad sudando sangre por nuestros pecados. Sus dicipulos no pudiéron velar ní una hora con El. Nuestro Senor no fué obligado a sufrir, fué su libre voluntad, por amor del uno al otro. Y asi entregó su vida humana para morir por nuestra salvación y por la vida eterna.

Tan grande fué su poder, escribió San Juan que cuando los Judios viniéron a prenderle y el les preguntó, Aquien Buscais? Respondiéronle, A Jesus Nazareno. Y al decirles, Yo soy, Caeron en tierra. Judas y los otros conocieron que habló, no un hombre sino Dios mismo. Cornelio tambien conoció esto despues de la crucificácion.

Tres veces preguntáron, A quien buscais. Nuestro Senor sabia todo esto. Nuestro señor que fué todo el tesoro, fué entregado por Judas, quién vino como una vipora, traidor y hipocrita, mostrandose como amigo, Más Jesus que conocía su intencion le dijo, "A que has venido?"

God in his mercy would have liked Judas to repent, as Peter would, what he had done, and for this purpose Jesus asked, "Why have you come?"

And so they captured Jesus for the way Judas used his unwashable lips. The injustice which would be perpetrated from that moment until Jesus' death can neither be imagined nor experienced.

THE PEOPLE SING:

> They have dragged him in chains
> And bound his arms;
> Past the cruel bonds
> The blood flows forth;
> And they bear him off a prisoner
> Like a man who has done wrong.

Taking him down the mountain with buffeting and other injuries, they came all the way from Gethsemane, while Jesus lost blood; they arrived at the house of Annas. Annas questioned him: "Tell me your secret doctrine."

Our Savior replied to him, "I have kept nothing hidden. I have shown the road to heaven. Why do you investigate me?" A bystander struck him a blow on the face.

What is his example to us? Well able to return blow for blow, able to kill, Jesus was godly and merely said, "Why do you strike me?"

They went with Our Lord to Caiphas, having reached no decision with Annas. They mocked him the whole way, the Jewish rabble. At the house of Caiphas all the council assembled. They provided many witnesses, but they contradicted one another, leaving no reason to condemn Jesus. But one of the priests asked him, "Are you the Son of God?"

Jesus replied, "Yes, I am."

"Blasphemy!" they cried, "he said he is the Son of God—enough evidence."

Do they really know the reason for this comedy? It is that the land has been conquered by the Romans, and it is necessary to take Christ before Pilate for him to pronounce sentence.

They do him injury and spit on him—spitting on this innocent man I cannot excuse.

THE PEOPLE SING:

> With a hand armed with iron
> On the innocent cheek
> They strike a blow so brutal
> That it makes the blood burst forth;
> My God, that a stubborn heart
> Should be the source of such harshness.

Dios en su misericordia ubiera querido que Judas se arrepintiera como Pedro lo habia hecho y por eso Jesus pregunto, "A qué has venido?"

Asi prendiéron a Nuestro Senor por los labios inlavables de Judás. No se puede imaginar ní experimentar la injusticia que hubo desde este momento hasta la muerte.

En la prisión lo arrastraron,
Y a los brazos con cordeles
Echando lazos crueles
La sangre le reventaron;
Y así preso lo llevaron
Como a un hombre malhechor.

Subieron al monte con golpes e injurias, fuéron a Jesemani, perdio sangre hasta llegar á la casa de Anas. Anas le pregunto, "Díme de tu doctrina secreta."

Nuestro Salvador le respondio, "Yo no hé hablado escondido. Ensenó el camino al cielo. Porqué me preguntas?" Uno que estaba ahí le dió un golpe en la cara o en el rostro.

Ejemplo, bien podía dar golpe por golpe, podía matar, pero fue justo y habló, "Porque me pegas?"

Se fuéron con Nuestro Senor a Caifas, no habiendo tenido resultado alguno con Anas. Burlas todo el camino, estos canallas de los judios. En casa de Caifas se juntáron todos los del concilio. Había muchos testigos pero se contradicéron y no halláron razón para condenarlo. Mas uno de los sacerdotes le pregunto, "Eres el Hijo de Dios?"

Jesus respondio, "Sí soy."

"Blasfemia!" gritáron, "Dice que es el Hijo de Dios, razón suficiente."

Désde ántes sabían porqué esta comedia? Porque el país estaba conquístado por los Romanos y era necesario llevarlo a Pilato para que él diera la sentencia.

Lo injuriáron y lo escupiéron pero escupir a un hombre inocente yo no halló escusa.

Con mano de hierro armada
A la mejilla inocente
Dan tan recia bofetada,
Que hacen que en sangre reviente,
Mi Dios, pues el alma siente
Ser causa de tal rigor.

Jesus' two friends, John and Peter, arrived at Caiphas' house and were allowed to enter. John had an acquaintance there and got Peter in, too. As Peter was sitting there, a maid came up to him and asked, "Do you know this man?"

But Peter denied it, saying, "I do not know him."

In the early morning he was with the soldiers and one of them asked him, "Are you also one of his followers?"

Peter answered, "Oh no, I am not."

Finally another of the soldiers said, "Surely, I have seen you with him."

Peter denied Christ for the third time and immediately the cock crowed.

Our Savior came out and a single glance was enough. Peter wept bitterly, and all his life he wept for repentance.

Meanwhile, Judas was able to repent of what he had done. He repented, though, in a merely natural manner, not supernaturally. He tried to give back the money but the council would not take it. Finally he threw the money into the temple. Money for blood! It is not a sin to sell things in business, but greed for money is a sin. A bad end it came to, that hypocrisy condemned by Our Lord.

Jesus sought solace from his heavenly father, and he sent an angel to console him.

(Here all kneel while the three little angels kneel and offer incense to Our Lord Jesus Christ, who is imprisoned in the jail.)

In the morning they took Our Lord to Pontius Pilate so he could ratify the unjust sentence for spreading the false doctrine of not paying taxes, false doctrines for which they sought to find him guilty. But he was giving us an example when he said, "Give to Caesar what belongs to Caesar, and give to God what belongs to God."

King! They wished to accuse him another time, and Pilate asked him, "Are you a king?"

He replied, "I am king; my kingdom is not of this world." Jesus did not have any soldiers, only blessings. Jesus was not a revolutionary.

Pilate spoke again and said, "I find no guilt in this man."

The Jews replied, "He has blasphemed God. And he is a revolutionary. He has come preaching false doctrine all the way from Galilee."

Hearing Galilee mentioned, Pilate was encouraged. He might be able to do something to avoid a decision, since the case came under the jurisdiction of Herod, a sensuous man who

Llegáron sus dos amigos, Juan y Pedro, y pudieron entrar. Juan conocía y llevó á Pedro. Y como Pedro estaba sentado, una criada llegó y le preguntó, "Conoces a este hombre?"

Más Pedro negó diciendo, "No sé lo que dices."

En la madrugada estubo alli adentro con los soldados y uno de ellos le dijo, "Tu fuiste tambien uno de ellos?"

Pedro respondio, "O no, yo no."

Entonces uno de los soldados dijo, "Seguro, yo lo he visto."

Pedro negó por tercera vez y luego el gallo cantó.

Salió Nuestro Salvador y una sola mirada fue suficiente. Pedro lloró amargamente y toda su vida lloró arrepentido.

Judás también podía haberse arrepentido. Si se arrepintió natural-mente peró no sobrenatural. El quizo entregar el dinero peró el concilio no lo acepto. Entonces él puso el dinero en el templo. Dinero de sangre! No es pecado vender en comercio, peró es pecado la avaricia por plata. Fue un mal fin por esta hipocracia que condenó a Nuestro Senor.

Jesus buscó consolacion en su padre celestial y El mando a un angel a consolarlo.

(Aqui se hincan todos mientras los tres angelitos le ofrecen incencio a Nuestro Senor Jesucristo, que está preso en la carcel.)

En la madrugada lleváron a Nuestro Senor a Poncio Pilato para conseguir la sentencia falsa, levantando falsas doctrinas que no pagaba tasación. Doctrinas falsas por que querían hallarle culpablo. Pero ejemplo nos dio cuando dijo, "Dar al César lo que es del César, y dar Diós lo que es de Diós."

Rey! Quisieron acusarle otra vez y Pilato le pregunto, "Eres rey?"

El respondió, "Soy rey, mi reino no es de este mundo." Jesus no tenia soldados, solo bienaventuranzas. Jesus no fué un revolucionario.

Pilato hablo entonces y dijo, "No halla culpa."

Los judios respondiéron, "Ha blasfemado á Diós. Si es revolucianario. Ha venido predicando doctrinas falsas desde Galilea."

Oyendo Pilato mencionar, Galilea, se alegró. Aquí si podía hacer algo porqué era de la jurisdicción de Herodes, hombre de

offered the head of John the Baptist and half his kingdom to the daughter of Herodias, with whom he lived in adultery.

Therefore Pilate sent Jesus to Herod. From this time on, Pilate and Herod were friends. Herod believed that Jesus could do miracles and called on him to do tricks and questioned him. But Jesus would not answer a word. Herod sent him back to Pilate with the message that the man must be out of his mind not to say anything.

This time Pilate recollected that he could pardon one man during the feast of the Passover. Pilate was sure that the crowd would prefer that he condemn Barabbas, and so he asked them, "Whom do you wish me to set free, this innocent and just man or that guilty man, that robber?"

The Jews cried, "Kill Jesus and free Barabbas!" Then Pilate delivered Jesus over to them and they began to mistreat him.

Holy Scripture says that his body was entirely one wound. They clothed him in purple and placed on his head a crown woven of thorns. They saluted him, "God save you, King of the Jews!"

THE PEOPLE SING:

> O, that someone had been there,
> My sweet lover and master,
> And the blow of each Jew
> Had taken on his face for your sake!
> All the guilt is mine alone
> But you have suffered for it, Lord.

Jesus Christ could have revenged himself, but he did not. He chose to suffer for us.

His example—infinite love for his neighbor. He sought like a good shepherd to lay down his life for his sheep.

"I have given you an example."

It is better to suffer unjustly than to think evil of our neighbor. Jesus Christ suffered patiently, ready to give up his life for our salvation.

In the name of the Father and of the Son and of the Holy Spirit, Amen.

Afterwards he gives his blessing.

lujo que ofrecio lá cabeza de San Juan Bautista y la mitad de su reino, a la hija de Herodias, con quíen vivía en adulterio.

Así Pilato despachó a Jesús á buscar á Herodes. Aquí formáron amistad Pilato y Herodes. Herodes creía que Jesus podía hacer milagros y lo vistió de burlas, y lo envestigó. Más Jesus no respondía nada. Volvió Herodes á llevárselo á Pilato diciendole este hombre está afuera del juicio no habla nada.

Otrz vez Pilato se recordó que podía perdonar a un hombre en cada fiesta. Pilato estaba seguro que la multitud quería que condenase mejor a Barrabas y por eso les preguntó, "A quién querreis que dé libre, á este hombre inocente y justo, o á este hombre delinquente, este ladrón?"

Los Judios gritáron, "Quitale á Jesús la vida y suéltanos a Barrabas!" Entonces Pilato les entregó á Jesus y ellos lo volviéron a maltratar.

Dice la sagrada escritura que todo su cuerpo era una sola llaga. Le vistiéron de purpura y le pusiéron una corona tejida de espinas. Saludandole, "Dios te salve rey de los Judios!"

> ¡Oh quién estuviera allí,
> Dulce amante y dueño mío,
> Y al golpe de aquel judío
> Pusiera el rostro por tí!
> Toda la culpa está en mí,
> Y Vos la pagáis, Señor.

Jesucristo podía vengárse peró no se vengo. El quería sufrir por nosotros.

Ejemplo—Amor a su projimo infinitum. El quizo como el Buen Pastor dar su vida por sus ovejas.

"Ejemplo Os He Dado."

Vale más padecer injustamente que condenar a nuestro projimo. Jesucrusto sufrió pacientemente, listo a dar su vida por nuestra salvación.

En el nombre del Padre, y del Hijo, y del Espirito Santo, Amen.

Despues la benedicion.

GOOD FRIDAY   APRIL 19, 1946

ACT THREE

SCENE ONE

The ceremony—at eight in the morning.
1. The Prophecy[15]
2. The unveiling of the Most Holy Cross.
3. The adoration of the Holy Cross.
4. The procession of the Three Falls.

Notes and explanations: During the adoration, the song "Venid O Cristianos" is sung.

---

15 *In the Holy Week services of the time, as they were practiced in Tomé, it would seem that Matins and Lauds may have been recited before Mass, and that this is what "The Prophecy" refers to. Otherwise, it would refer to the first two readings of the Mass (Hosea 6 and Exodus 12). The unveiling and adoration of the Cross are part of the ceremonies of the Mass of the Presanctified (so called because there is no consecration; the host used is from the previous day).*

"VENID, O CRISTIANOS"

Come, O Christians,
Let us adore the cross,
Let us adore the cross
Which has saved the world.

Happy the soul
That keeps it in mind,
Who with burning
Devotion loves it.

Come, faithful souls,
Kiss with longing
The key to heaven,
The cross of the Lord.

VIERNES SANTO   ABRIL 19, 1946

ACTO TERCERO

ESCENA PRIMERA

Los oficios—A las 8:00 de la mañana.
1. La Profecia.
2. El descubrimiento de la Santisima Cruz.
3. Adoracion de la Santa Cruz.
4. La procesion de Las Tres Caidas.

Notas y explicaciones: Para la adoracion se canta "Venid O Cristianos."

"VENID O CRISTIANOS"

Venid, O Cristianos,
La cruz adoremos,
La Cruz ensalcemos
Que al mundo salvo.

Dichosa aquella alma,
Que tiene presente
A quien con ardiente
Affecto la amo.

Venid, almas fieles,
Besad con anhelo
La llave del cielo,
La cruz del Senor.

Receive me, Holy Cross,
My arms are tired,
And reclining on you
Let them reach to God.

Whoever seeing you lifeless
Hanging on the cross
The victim of our sins,
Sees you die, Good Jesus.

My beloved Jesus,
How often I have offended you,
Pardon my transgressing,
And have mercy on me.

* * *

GOOD FRIDAY   APRIL 19, 1946

SCENE TWO

THE PROCESSION OF THE THREE FALLS

PERSONAGES

The Most Holy Cross ....Carried by Crestino Baca.

The Centurion—(on a roan horse) ....Ramón Chavira.

The Jews ....the same as in Act Two.

The leader of the Jews ....Don Estevan Torrez.

The leaders of the procession ....Elauterio Sanchez,
Juan Estevan Zamora.

Pontius Pilate ....Adelino Sanchez

Pilate's servant ....Fred Landavazo, Jr.

Judas ....Prudencio Marquez

Recibe, Cruz Santa,
Mis brazos cansados,
Y en ti reclinados
Alcansen a Dios.

Quien al mirarte exanime
Pendiente de una cruz
Por nuestras culpas victima,
Expirar, Buen Jesus.

Amante Jesus mio,
O cuanto te ofendi,
Perdonami mi estravio,
Y ten piedad de mi.

* * *

VIERNES SANTO   ABRIL 19, 1946

ESCENA SEGUNDA

LA PROCESION DE LAS TRES CAIDAS

PERSONAJES

La Santisima Cruz ....Llevada por Crestino Baca.

El Centurion—(caballo colorado) ....Ramon Chavira.

Los Judios ....Los mismos del segundo acto.

El jefe de los Judios ....Don Estevan Torrez.

Los directores de la procesion ....Elauterio Sanchez,
Juan Estevan Zamora

Poncio Pilatos ....Adelino Sanchez

El criado del Pilatos ....Fred Landavazo, Jr.

Judas ....Prudencio Marquez

Barabbas ....Pilar Moya

Three little angels ....the same as in Act Two.
(they carry the crown, the nails, and
the hammer)

The Divine Image ....carried by: Pat Sanchez, Fred Landavazo,
Esmael Sanchez, Andres A. Córdova

An official ....Pablo Lucero

A Jew, who loads the cross of Our Lord ....Elias Chavira

Mary Most Holy—(Our Lady of Sorrows) ....carried by:
Mrs. Perfecto Moya, Mrs. Juan Estevan Zamora,
Mrs. Castulo Moya, Mrs. Antonia Mirabal

Saint John ......carried by: Serefino Sanchez, Nicanor Sanchez

Simon of Cyrene ....Tobias Lucero.

Veronica ....Mrs. Lucia Lucero

The Holy Women of Jerusalem ....Mrs. Macedonio Gurule,
Mrs. Pablo Lucero, Mrs. Teofilo Baca,
Mrs. Doroteo Baca, Mrs. Toribio Chavez,
Mrs. Francisco Vallejos

The Servers
The Priest   (the same as in previous acts.)
The choir

THE PROCESSION OF THE THREE FALLS

This scene begins at the front of the church, moves in
procession through the plaza, and ends with a sermon in front of
the church.

It begins at nine in the morning.

In the facade of the church there is a balcony which
represents the palace of Pilate where Our Lord Jesus Christ is
sentenced to death. Pilate is seated on a throne on the balcony,

Barabbas . . . . .Pilar Moya

Tres angelitos . . . . .Los mismos del acto segundo.
                (llevan la corona, los clavos, el martillo)

El Divino Rostro . . . . .Llevado por:
                Pat Sanchez, Fred Landavazo,
            Esmael Sanchez, Andres A. Cordova.

Un oficial . . . . .Pablo Lucero

Un judio, que le carga la cruz a Nuestro Senor . . .Elias Chavira

Maria Santisima—(Nuestra Senora de los Dolores) . .Llevada por:
           Sra. Perfecto Moya, Sra. Juan Estevan Zamora,
            Sra. Castulo Moya, Sra. Antonia Mirabal

San Juan . . . . .Llevado por: Seferino Sanchez, Nicanor Sanchez

Simon Cirineo . . . . .Tobias Lucero.

La Veronica . . . . .Sra. Lucia Lucero

Las Piadosas Mujeres . . . . .Sra. Macedonio Gurule,
             Sra. Pablo Lucero, Sra. Teofilo Baca,
          Sra. Doroteo Baca, Sra. Toribio Chavez,
                Sra. Francisco Vallejos

Los sacristanes
El Sacerdote   (Los mismos de los actos anteriores.)
El coro

LA PROCESION DE LAS TRES CAIDAS

El escenario toma lugar afuera de la iglesia, por la plaza y despues el sermon adelante de la iglesia.

    Tiempo las 9:00 de la manana.

    En el frente de la iglesia hay un balcon que representa la casa de Pilatos donde Nuestro Senor Jesucristo fue sentenciado a muerte. Pilatos esta sentado en un sillon en el balcon y abajo

and beneath[17] the balcony are Barabbas in shackles and chains and the Jews.

The people file out of the church and form into various lines together.

Jesus Christ is brought before[18] Pilate.

There is read the prayer of the FIRST STATION, Jesus is condemned to death.

All the people kiss the ground and say (at each station): "We adore thee O Christ and we bless thee, Because by thy holy cross thou hast redeemed the world."

The priest reads: "Contemplate, my soul, in this first station, what sort of place the palace of Pilate is, where the redeemer of the world was cruelly crowned with thorns and sentenced to death."

The people respond (at each station): "Blessed and praised forever be the Lord so great."

Then Pilate speaks to the people, saying:

Pilate.—Jesus of Nazareth is innocent; I find no guilt at all in this man.

Jews.—He is guilty. Condemn him to the cross!

The leader alone.—He is an enemy of Caesar! He is a disturber of the republic, and a spreader of false doctrines!

All the Jews.—To the cross!

Pilate.—Whom do you wish [me to release], Jesus, an innocent, gentle, and just man, or this despicable man, this lawbreaker, this criminal Barabbas?

The leader alone.—Destroy the life of Jesus and set Barabbas free!

All the Jews.—Long live Barabbas!

(At this point a Roman soldier removes the chains from Barabbas and hangs them on the railing in view of all the people, and Barabbas goes to join the rest of the Jews.)

(And now a boy offers Pilate water and he washes his hands.)

Pilate.—I am innocent of the blood of this just man.

The leader alone.—Let his blood fall upon us and upon our children!

And now Pilate reads the sentence in a loud voice:

---

17 The movie shows Barabbas on the balcony with Pilate.
18 Christ is brought out the church door below.

del balcon está Barrabas en grios y cadenas y los judios.

Sale la gente de la iglesia y forman varias filas en grupo.

Jesu Cristo es llevado delante Pilato.

Se resa la PRIMERA ESTACION, Jesus es condenado a muerte.

Besan todos la tierra y decen (en cada estacion): Adoramoste, Cristo, y bendecimoste. Que por tu santa cruz redimiste al mundo.

El Sacerdote lee: Contempla, alma, en esta primera estacion, que es la casa de Pilatos, donde fue rigurosamente el Redentor del mundo, coronado de espinas y sentenciado a muerte.

La gente responde (en cada estacion): Bendito y alabado sea para siempre tan gran Senor.

En seguida habla Pilato al pueblo y dice asi:

Pilato.—Jesus de Nazareno es innocente, no hallo culpa alguna en este Hombre.

Judios.—Es Culpable. Condenalo a la cruz!

Jefe solo.—Es el enemigo del Caesar! Inquietador de las Republicas, y sembrador de doctrinas falsas!

Judios todos.—A la cruz!

Pilato.—A quien quereis, A Jesus el hombre inocente, manso y justo, o a este hombre vil, este reo, este criminal Barrabas?

Jefe solo.—Quitale a Jesus la vida y sueltanos libre a Barrabas!

Judios todos.—Viva Barrabas!

(Aqui un soldado Romano le quita la cadena a Barrabas y la cuelga en el balcon a vista de todo el pueblo, y Barrabas se junta con todos los demas Judios)

(Aqui un nino le echa el agua a Pilato y el se lava las manos.)

Pilato.—Inocente soy de la sangre de este justo.

Jefe solo.—Que caiga su Sangre sobre nosotros y sobre nuestros hijos!

Aqui Pilato lee la sentencia con voz fuerte:

THE SENTENCE[19]

I, Pontius Pilate, president of Lower Galilee, this day the 25th of March in the year 5001 from the creation of the world, hand over and sentence Jesus, named for his town the Nazarene, to be crucified on a cross, and placed between two thieves, Dismas and Gestas (already sentenced to death), one on his right and the other on his left on the mountain called Golgotha, as a false prophet, a deceiver of the people, a disturber of the republic, a spreader of false doctrines and a necromancer, who in league with devils does supposed miracles, working to achieve the goals of Beelzebub prince of Hell, and like a tyrant is usurping kingdoms and betraying Caesar the emperor of the Romans. And furthermore I decree to our centurion Quintus Cornelius that he shall lead him through all the streets of Jerusalem with a herald going ahead and crying out all the misdeeds of this criminal, so he may be an example to all the people, and that he pass by the courthouse[20] where my sentence should be read. Moreover I ordain that there be placed atop the cross a sign reading thus: "Jesus of Nazareth King of the Jews," which should be written in three languages, Hebrew, Greek, and Latin, so that all may read and understand.

This is our will; done and concluded on the date aforesaid in our palace.

Pontius Pilate, President

Notes and explanations: Copied 12 March 1947 from a copy made 25 March 1910, from a baptismal register which had been brought from Mexico.

---

19 There are at least three versions of the decree; they differ in no main points. Another carries the date 18 November 1905.

20 This is the old courthouse on the Tomé square; the town was county seat during the last century.

LA SENTENCIA

Yo, Poncio Pilato, presidente de la inferior Galilea, hoy dia 25 de marzo, del ano 5001 de la creacion del mundo, mando y sentencio a Jesus, llamado por el pueblo Nazareno, que sea crucificado en una cruz, y puesto entre dos ladrones, Dimas y Gestas, ya sentenciados a muerte, el uno a la diestra y el otro a la siniestra en el monte llamado Golgota, como falso profeta, enganador de las gentes, enquietador de las republicas, sembrador de doctrinas falsas y negromatico, que con pacto con los demonios obra fingidos milagros, valiendose para ello de Beelzebub principe del infierno, y como tirano usurpador de reinos y traidor al Cesar emperador de los Romanos. Y tambien mando a nuestro centurion Quinto Cornelio, que lo pasee en todas las calles de Jerusalem, con un pregonero que vaya adelante gritando todas las maldades del reo, para que sirva de ejemplo a todo el pueblo, y pasara por la puerta judiciaria, donde sera leida alli mi sentencia. Ademas ordeno que sea puesto un retulo arriba de la cruz que rese asi: Jesus Nazareno Rey de los Judios, el cual sera escrito en tres idiomas, Hebraica, Griega, y Latina, esto es para que todos la puedan leer y entender;—

Esta es nuestra voluntad; hecho y firmado en la fecha arriba mencionada en nuestro palacio.

Poncio Pilatos Presidente

Notas y explicaciones: Copiada 12 de marzo de 1947 de una copia hecha el 25 de marzo de 1910 del libro de registro de bautizmo que tuvieron a Mejico.

Pilate.—We here declare forfeit the emblem of this condemned man.

Now a soldier breaks the token, a small staff. Next, one of the Roman soldiers places the document on the lance of the centurion on horseback, who now leads off the procession with a great show of ceremony.

The priest continues with the rest of the Way of the Cross. The Roman soldiers go ahead of the crowd of the Jews. Pilate leaves his balcony and enters his palace.

Notes and explanations: In the afternoon all the Jews follow behind; that is to say, following the Holy Body, and the Roman soldiers go ahead and guard the Holy Body of Jesus.

After these reenactments have been concluded in the churchyard, the procession begins.

The centurion leads (on his roan horse)
The Holy Cross
Jesus Christ
The official   Mary Magdalen
The soldiers
The Jews
From the other direction to encounter Jesus come:
The Most Holy Virgin and Saint John
Simon of Cyrene
Veronica
The holy women of Jerusalem.

In turning toward the east side of the plaza, the people form four lines on each side and here they pray the second station.

SECOND STATION, Jesus takes the cross on his shoulders.

"Contemplate, my soul, at this second station, what the place is like where our beloved Jesus raises onto his injured shoulders the heavy weight of the cross."

Here they lay the cross upon Our Lord's shoulder.

All walk on a little further.

THIRD STATION, Jesus falls the first time.

"Contemplate, my soul, at this third station, what the place is like where the Lord, laboring with the cross up the hills, groaning and sighing, falls to the earth beneath the holy cross."

Pilato.—Tomamos aqui el baston de este condenado.

Aqui un soldado quiebra el baston. En seguida uno de los soldados Romanos pone la sentencia en la lanza de Centurion y este se va adelante de la procesion en su caballo con brio y pompa.

Sigue el sacerdote con las estaciones del Via Cruces. Los soldados Romanos adelante de la turba de Judios. Pilato se retira del balcon y entra en su casa.

Notas y explicaciones: En la tarde los judios todos van atras, es dicir siguiendo el Santo Cuerpo, y los soldados Romanos adelante guardiando el Santo Cuerpo de Jesus.

Despues de que estas representaciones han terminado adelante de la iglesia sigue la procesion.

El centurion adelante (caballo colorado)

La Santa Cruz

Jesucristo

El oficial   La Magdalena

Los soldados

Los judios

Por el otro lado a encontrar a Jesucristo van:

La Santisima Virgen y San Juan

Simon Sirineo

La Veronica

Las piadosas mujeres.

Al voltear al lado oriente de la plaza la gente forman cuatro filas de cada lado y aqui se resa la segunda estacion.

SEGUNDA ESTACION, Jesus con la cruz a cuestas.

"Contempla, alma, en esta segunda estacion, como es el lugar donde a nuestro amado Jesus le pusieron en sus lastimados hombros el grave peso de la cruz."

Aqui le cargan la cruz a Nuestro senor.

Caminan todos poco mas adelante.

TERCERA ESTACION, Jesus cae la primera vez.

"Contempla, alma, en esta tercera estacion, como es el lugar donde caminando el Señor con la cruz a cuestas, gimiendo y suspirando, cayo en tierra, y debajo de la santa cruz."

Here the Lord falls for the first time beneath the holy cross.

The men who walk in front carrying the statue of the Lord genuflect, and the Lord appears to fall.

All walk on a little further.

"ACOMPANEMOS AL CALVARIO"

Let us go to Calvary,
O Christians, to our Redeemer
Weeping for our sins
Which are the cause of his sorrow.

Mary, sorrowful Mother,
The wounds of my Redeemer
Engrave in my heart.

O Jesus, the fatal sentence
Which Pilate pronounced on you;
For me, a vile criminal, patiently
You suffered it to redeem me.[21]

Innocent, the deadly tree
Why did you wish to carry, my Savior?
I, a criminal, deserve only
That you treat me with great severity.

Beneath such a weighty burden
Falling, the Lord did not complain;
The sacred model of patience—
Imitate him, oh sinful man.

Where are you hurrying, loving Mother?
Stop yourself, or the sword of grief
At the sight of the blood of your Son
Will pierce your heart.

---

21 *The present stanza and the next thirteen each takes one Station of the Cross.*

Aqui caee el Señor por primera vez degajo de la santa cruz.

Los hombres que van adelante con el Senor se hincan y el Senor parece caer.

Caminan todos un poco mas.

ACOMPANEMOS AL CALVARIO[22]

Acompañemos al Calvario,
Oh Cristianos, a nuestro Redentor,
Llorando por nuestros pecados,
Que causa son de su dolor.

María, Madre de dolor,
Las llagas de mi Redentor
Grabad en mi corazón

Oh Jesús, la mortal sentencia
Que pronunció Pilato contra Vos.
Por mí, vil reo, con paciencia
La sufrís por mi redención.

Inocente el fatal madero
¿Por qué queréis cargar, mi Salvador?
Yo criminal sólo merezco
Me tratéis con tanto rigor.

Bajo tan riguroso peso
Sucumbiendo, no se queja el Señor;
De paciencia santo modelo,
Imitadlo, hombre pecador.

¿Do corréis, tiernísima Madre?
Deteneos, la espada de dolor,
Al ver de vuestro hijo la sangre,
Traspasa vuestro corazón.

---

22 *The first three syllables of the fourth line of each stanza (though not of the chorus) are repeated; the three-line chorus is repeated after each stanza.*

Your aid, weak Cyrenian,
The Lord Creator does not disdain;
To our brothers we all ought
To bring help for love of you.

Blessed Veronica, your zeal
Deserves its precious reward:
For of the divine face your veil
Preserves the sweet likeness.

Jesus falls the second time
Beneath the cross, tired and sorrowful;
Let our relapses into sin
Be cured by your divine love.

Holy women, your weeping
Consoles him; Jesus teaches us
That it is vain to weep if by sin
We wound the Lord himself.

Let us press our faces to the earth--
The Savior falls the third time--
At the sight of his sleepless captivity
Mocked by sinful men.

Cover, angels, with your wings
The cruel nakedness of the God-Man;
For you, oh unchaste souls,
His countenance blushes for shame.

To expiate the foolish abuse
Of your free will and reason,
See, sinner, see the just God
Nailed like a common thief.

The sign on Calvary
Lifted for our redemption,
O victim of my salvation,
Draw my heart to yourself.

Tu apoyo, débil Cirineo,
No desdeña el Soberano Hacedor:
A nuestros hermanos debemos
Socorrerlos por vuestro amor.

Feliz Verónica, tu celo
Te merece precioso galardón:
Del divino rostro tu velo
Conserva la dulce impresión.

Cae Jesús la segunda vez,
Bajo la cruz con fatiga y dolor:
Nuestras criminales recaídas
Remedia su divino amor.

Mujeres pías, vuestro llanto
Consolando, Jesús nos enseñó
Que es vano llorar, si pecando
Herimos al mismo Señor.

Postremos la frente en el suelo,
Tercera vez cae el Salvador,
Al ver su prisión y desvelos
Burlados por el pecador.

Cubrid, ángeles, con las alas
La desnudez cruel del Hombre-Dios,
Por vos, oh deshonestas almas,
La frente sufre con rubor.

Para expiar el insensato abuso
De tu libre arbitrio y razón,
Ved, pecador, ved al Dios justo
Clavado como vil ladrón.

El estandarte en el Calvario
Enarbolan de nuestra redención:
Oh víctima de mi rescate,
Atraéos mi corazón.

The sacrifice is finished,
They lower the dead Savior;
See him stiff and wounded—
O Mother, how great your sorrow!

To lighten, oh mortal, your fate,
The sovereign Lord of life
See submit to the tomb;
He will be your resurrection.

Sinner, the passion and death
Which the Son of God suffered for you
Will be for you, if you do not change,
The cause of greater sorrow.

FOURTH STATION, Jesus meets his mother.
"Contemplate, my soul, at this fourth station, what the place is like where Our Lord, walking with the cross up the hill, encountered his most holy Mother in her sorrow and affliction."

Here Mary Most Holy encounters Christ as Saint John follows her. The women who carry her and the men who carry the Lord approach one another and Mary Most Holy and Jesus Christ embrace. Subsequently, Mary Most Holy and Saint John follow the Lord.

Everyone goes on a little further forward.

FIFTH STATION, Simon of Cyrene helps Jesus carry the cross.

"Contemplate, my soul, at this fifth station, what the place is like where [the soldiers] conscript Simon of Cyrene to help our Redeemer carry the cross; they are moved not by pity but by fear he will die on the way because of the great weight of the cross."

Here Simon of Cyrene, who had come with his two sons, is forced by two soldiers to help carry our Redeemer's cross. Simon takes the cross and carries it.

All go forward.

SIXTH STATION, Veronica wipes the face of Jesus.

"Contemplate, my soul, at this sixth station, what the place is like where the woman Veronica, seeing Jesus so tired, and with his face covered with perspiration, dust, spittle, and blood from the abuse he has received, offers a linen cloth with which she wipes his face."

120

El sacrificio consumado,
Inánime bajan al Salvador:
Yerto viéndole y vulnerado,
Oh Madre, ¿cuál fué tu dolor?

Para aliviar, mortal, tu suerte,
De la vida el soberano Señor
Ved al sepulcro someterse;
El será tu resurrección.

Pecador, la pasión y muerte
Que padeció por ti el Hijo de Dios,
Te será, si no te conviertes,
La causa de pena mayor.

CUARTA ESTACION, Jesus encuentra a su madre.
"Contempla, alma, en esta cuarta estacion, como es el lugar donde caminando el Señor con la santa cruz a cuestas, se encontro con su santisima Madre triste y afligida."

Aqui Maria Santisima encuentra al Senor San Juan la sigue. Las senoras que la llevan y los hombres que traen al Senor se acercan y Maria Santisima y Jesucristo se abrazan. Despues Maria Santisima y San Juan siguen al Senor.

Caminan todos poco mas adelante.

QUINTA ESTACION, El cirineo ayuda a Jesus a llevar la cruz.
"Contempla, alma, en esta quinta estacion, como es el lugar donde alquilaron a Simon Cireneo para que ayudase a llevar la cruz a nuestro Redentor, no movidos de piedad, sino temiendo se les muriese en el camino por el peso grande de la cruz."

Aqui Simon Cireneo quien viene con sus do hijos es prendido por dos soldados para que ayude a llevar la cruz a nuestro Redentor. Simon Cireneo toma la cruz y la lleva.

Caminan todos.

SEXTA ESTACION, La Veronica limpia el rostro de Jesus.
"Contempla, alma en esta sexta estacion, como es el lugar donde la mujer Veronica, viendo a Jesus tan fatigado, y su rostro oscurecido por el sudor, polvo, salivas, bofetadas que dieron, se quito un lienzo con que le limpio."

EL LIENZO DE LA VERONICA

Here Veronica, who comes forward with a folded cloth, wipes the sweat from our Savior. Then she shows it to everyone with the visage of the Lord imprinted on it.

All go forward, with Veronica holding her cloth ahead of Jesus Christ.[23]

SEVENTH STATION,[24] Jesus falls the second time.

"Contemplate, my soul, at this seventh station, how it is at this place outside the courthouse[25] where the Lord falls the second time and has opened in his shoulder a large and deadly wound."

Here Our Lord falls the second time. The men who walk at the front of the pallet kneel and the Lord seems to fall.

All proceed.

EIGHTH STATION, Jesus consoles the holy women.

"Contemplate, my soul, at the eighth station, what the place is like where various holy women, seeing the Lord going out to be crucified, weep bitterly to see him so badly wounded."

Here the holy women encounter Our Lord. Afterwards, they walk behind the Virgin and Saint John.

All go forward.

NINTH STATION, Jesus falls the third time.

"Contemplate, my soul, at this ninth station, what the place is like where the Lord falls to the earth for the third time, so that he lies with his sacred mouth against the dirt. Attempting to rise, he cannot, until he even falls anew."

Here the Lord falls for the third time. They force him to raise himself, but he only falls again.

All proceed.

Here everyone arrives back in front of the church and gather at random on one side and the other.

The priest preaches the sermon on the Three Falls.

---

23 According to informants, "Mi Dios y Mi Redentor" was sung during the procession. For the text, see above.

24 Mr. Ben M. Otero's narrative and movie both suggest very explicitly that the usual seventh and eighth stations as given here are reversed so that the final two falls come together.

25 This is the courthouse mentioned above.

Aqui la Veronica Quien viene con un lienzo doblado le limpia el sudor a nuestro Redentor. Despues lo muestra a todos y el Senor esta impreso en el.

Caminan todos, la Veronica con el lienzo adelante de Jesucristo.

SEPTIMA ESTACION, Jesus cae por segunda vez.

"Contempla, alma, en esta septima estacion, como es el lugar de la puerta Judiciaria, en donde cayo el Senor segunda vez, por abersele hecho en el hombro una llaga muy grande y mortal."

Aqui cae nuestro Senor por segunda vez. Los hombres de adelante que lo llevan se hincan y el Senor parece caer.

Caminan todos.

OCTAVA ESTACION, Jesus consuela a las piadosas mujeres.

"Contempla, alma, en esta octava estacion, como es el lugar donde unas piadosas mujeres, viendo al Senor que llevaban a crucificar, lloraron amargamente de verle tan injuriado."

Aqui las piadosas mujeres encuentran a nuestro Senor. Despues caminan detras de la Virgen y San Juan.

Caminan todos.

NOVENA ESTACION, Jesus cae por tercera vez.

"Contempla, alma, en esta novena estacion, como es el lugar donde cayo el Senor tercera vez en tierra, hasta llegar con su santa boca en el suelo, y queriendose levantar no pudo, antes volvio a caer de nuevo."

Aqui cae el Senor por tercera vez. Hace fuerza levantarse y cae de nuevo.

Caminan todos.

Aqui llegan todos a frents de la iglesia y se afilan envarias filas a un lado y otro.

El sacerdote da el sermon de las Tres Caidas.

A SERMON ON THE THREE FALLS OF CHRIST
BY THE REVEREND FATHER JOSE ASSENMACHER
NINE IN THE MORNING—GOOD FRIDAY

In the name of the Father and of the Son and of the Holy Spirit, amen.

I HAVE GIVEN YOU AN EXAMPLE.

With a heavy heart, Jesus Christ suffered to teach us the path of truth. Christ himself was the path, the path of the cross. If there is a royal road, I know of only one, that which the Divine Heart followed from his birth to the cross. Follow Our Savior, who chose to suffer of his own free will. If I wish to follow him, I must follow a painful road indeed. Our Lord traveled that road.

It has been simply said that the people made their choice between sin and truth, between a man and a murderer. They chose to see Barabbas go free and to crucify Jesus. And so he walked that sorrowful road, weighed down and covered with blood. It was no straight path but one tortuous and rocky. Our Lord almost fainted, for he had lost much blood traveling up Calvary, so mistreated and spit upon. Worn out and already without much strength, he stumbled over a stone and fell under the cross.

We do not know how many times he fell for certain, but we commemorate three falls. Our Lord fell for us, he fell three times for our repeated sins. Walking along with that dismal entourage, fatigued and sorrowful, toward Calvary. Alone, for his friends had abandoned him. His mother did not forget him and did not abandon him. On the way Jesus Christ met his mother. What sorrow!

He was nothing beautiful, but instead a man fainting, covered with blood, mistreated, his face bloodstained.

Look at Jesus! Do you want to serve him and avoid sin?

In the fifth station, the Jews, seeing that Our Lord was nearly fainting from the heavy weight of the cross, not wishing him to die on the way since they wanted him to die on the cross, conscripted Simon of Cyrene to help carry the cross.

It was nothing he wanted to do, but he was rewarded for it. God rewarded him generously, softening his heart so that Simon died a great saint. Thus it is that Jesus rewarded him.

If the road of the cross is a very burdensome journey, God helps you to bear it as Jesus Christ and Simon did going to Golgotha.

SERMON DE LAS TRES CAIDAS
POR EL REVERENDO PADRE JOSE ASSENMACHER
TIEMPO—VIERNES SANTO A LAS 9:00 DE LA MANANA

En el nombre del Padre y del Hijo Y del Espirito Santo Amen.

EJEMPLO OS HE DADO.

Bajo este moto, Nuestro Senor Jesucristo padecio para ensenarnos el camino de la verdad. Cristo mismo fue el camino de la cruz. Si hay un camino real, yo conozco solo uno, el que el Corazon Divino siguio desde su nacimiento hasta la cruz. Seguir a Nuestro salvador, El quizo sufrir pues fue su voluntad. Si yo te quiero seguro, debo seguir un camino doloroso. Nuestro Senor camino este camino.

Han oido en simple forma como la gente tenia su eleccion entre el pecado y la verdad. Entre un hombre o un matador. Quisieron mejor ver libre a Barrabas y crucificar a Jesus. Asi comenzo este camino doloroso, pesado y marcado de sangre. No era un camino derecho sino un camino torcido y pedregoso. Nuestro Senor casi desmallado, porque perdia mucha sangre, caminaba asi al Monte Calvario, maltratado y escupido. Fatigado ya casi sin fuerza tropeso con un penasco y callo con la cruz.

No sabemos de cierto cuantas veces callo pero si hay tres caidas. Nuestro Senor callo por nosotros, tres veces por los repetidos pecados. Asi caminando con triste plebe, fatigado y desolado a el Calvario. Solo, porque sus amigos le abandonaron. Su madre no le olvido y no le abandono. En el camino Jesucristo encontro a su madre. Que dolor!

No fue una vista, fue un hombre casi desmallado, cubierto de sangre, maltratado, su rostro sangriento.

Mira a Jesus! Quieres servirle y evitar el pecado?

En esta quinta estacion los Judios viendo que Nuestro Senor casi desmallado por el grave peso de la cruz, no queriendo que se les muriese en el camino por que querian que muriera en la cruz, alquilaron a Simon Sirineo para que le ayudara a llevar la cruz.

Fue involuntariamente pero si tambien fue pagado. Dios pago bien. Ablando su corazon y Simon murio como un gran santo. Asi pago Jesus.

Si el camino de la cruz es un camino muy pesado, Dios te ayuda a llevarla como Jesucristo y Simon la llevaron a Golgota.

Jesus knew the human heart. One day they brought him a woman accused of having lived in adultery. They asked him, "What do you say?" The hypocrites did not know Jesus.

Jesus answered, "Whoever of you is without sin, let him be the one to throw the first stone." Nobody dared to. Finally Jesus said to the woman, "Go in peace and sin no more." Words of consolation, not of condemnation.

The woman did not forget. When Our Savior came with the cross she wiped the dust and sweat from his holy face. Today we still remember Veronica in the Church.[26]

This is the royal road. Learn from Christ's example. It is a divine road and today in the sacrifice of the mass Jesus Christ honors us with his presence only to redeem us from our sins.

From this day forward it does not matter what your road is, but imitate: I HAVE GIVEN YOU AN EXAMPLE.

In the name of the Father and of the Son and of the Holy Spirit, amen.

At the end of the sermon the statues are carried inside the church.

GOOD FRIDAY   APRIL 19, 1946

SCENE THREE

THE SERMON OF THE DEPOSITION

PERSONAGES

The Priest
The Servers
The choir

(The same as in previous acts.)
They sing "Perdón O Diós Mio."

Our Lady of Sorrows

Saint John

---

26 *The identification of the woman taken in adultery (John 8:3-11) with Veronica (from Christian folklore) is uncommon.*

Jesus conocia los corazones. Un dia la presentaron a una mujer acusandola de que vivia en adulterio. Le preguntaron, "Que dices tu?" Hipocritas no conocian a Jesus.

Jesus les responddio, "Quien de vosotros es sin pecado? Ese que tire la primer pedrada." Ninguno se atrevio. Entonces Jesus le dijo a la mujer, "Vete en paz y no peques mas." Palabras de consolacion, no de condenacion.

Esta mujer no olvido esto. Cuando Nuestro Senor iba con la cruz ella le limpio el polvo y sudor de su santo rostro. Hoy recordamos a la Veronica en la Iglesia.

Asi es el camino real. Tomad ejemplo. Es un camino divino y hoy en el sacrificio de la misa Jesucristo nos honrra con su presencia solo por redemir nuestros pecados.

De hoy en adelante no importa cual tu camino es—imitar: EJEMPLO OS HE DADO.

En el nombre del Padre y del Hijo y del Espirito Santo Amen.

Terminado el sermon se llevan las estatues para adentro de la iglesia.

VIERNES SANTO   ABRIL 19, 1946

ESCENA TERCERA

EL SERMON DEL DECENDIMIENTO

PERSONAJES

El Sacerdote
Los sacristanes
El coro

(Los mismos de los actos anteriores.)
Se canta: "Perdón O Dios Mio."

Nuestra Senora de los dolores.

San Juan.

NUESTRA SEÑORA
DE LOS DOLORES

LA SANGRE DE CRISTO

The persons beneath the cross ....Tobias Lucero,
José Orona, Mrs. Antonio Baca,
Mrs. Frank Baca, Mrs. Frank Montoya,
Mrs. Daniel Lucero, Mrs. Elias Romero

Joseph and Nicodemus ....Pablo Lucero, Nick Sanchez

The Lord Nailed to the Cross[27] (and afterwards)

The Holy Body—in the coffin .....carried by: Henrique Garley,
Eloy Garley, Francisco Baca,
Ventura Sanchez, Castulo Moya,
Andrés Romero

The Centurion ....Ramón Chavira

Blind Longinus ....Frank Montoya

The man who carries the table ....Juan Barela

The people who walk in the procession

The soldiers guarding the Holy Body

The Jews, who follow the Holy Body.

---

27 The 1946 enactment from which this text derives staged the crucifixion
in the church, and there was only the one cross; when the Memorial
Monument was built (and even in 1947) the parts of Dismas and Gestas (the
good thief and the bad) were added, and were first played by Trinidád Torrez
and Juan Torrez, each then about fourteen years old.

La gente que esta debajo de la Cruz . . . . .Tobias Lucero,
Jose Orona, Sra. Antonio Baca,
Sra. Frank Baca, Sra. Frank Montoya,
Sra. Daniel Lucero, Sra. Elias Romero

Jose y Nicodemos . . . . .Pablo Lucero, Nick Sanchez

El Senor Clavado en la cruz despues el

Santo Entierro—en la urna . . . . . .Llevada por: Henrique Garley,
Eloy Garley, Francisco Baca,
Ventura Sanchez, Castulo Moya,
Andres Romero

El Centurion . . . . .Ramon Chavira

El Ciego Longino . . . . .Frank Montoya

Un Hombre que lleva la mesa . . . . .Juan Barela

La gente que va en la procecion.

Los Soldados guardiando el Santo Cuerpo.

Los Judios Que van siguiendo el Santo Cuerpo.

THE SERMON ON THE DEPOSITION

The action takes place at the main altar and afterwards during the procession around the plaza.

It begins at three in the afternoon.

The altar is covered with a black curtain; in front of this is another curtain, this one white.

The Priest and the Servers enter.

They pray the following stations of the Way of the Cross:

TENTH STATION, Jesus is stripped of his garments.

"Contemplate, my soul, at this tenth station, what the place is like where, having led the Lord to the hill of Calvary, they strip him and give him to drink wine mixed with gall."

ELEVENTH STATION, Jesus is nailed to the cross.

"Contemplate, my soul, in this eleventh station, what the place is like where the Lord was nailed to the cross; and hearing the first stroke of the hammer, this most holy Mother is as it were stricken to death by her sorrow. Then the soldiers replace the crown of thorns with great cruelty and brutality."

Before the sermon they sing "Perdón O Dios Mio."

"PERDON, O DIOS MIO"

Pardon, O my God,
Pardon, forgiveness,
Pardon and clemency,
Pardon and mercy.

I sinned; yes my soul
Confesses her guilt,
A thousand times I grieve over
Such enormous evil.

A thousand times I regret
That my having sinned
Tore open your breast,
O supreme goodness.

EL SERMON DEL DECENDIMIENTO

El escenario toma lugar en el altar mayor y despues la procesion por la plaza.

Tiempo a las 3:00 de la tarde.

El altar esta cubierto con una cortina negra. Adelante de esta hay otra cortina blanca.

Entran el Sacerdote y los Sacristanes.

Se resan las siguiente estaciones del Via Crucis:

DECIMA ESTACION, Jesus es desposado de sus vestiduras.

"Contempla, alma, en esta decima estacion, como es el lugar donde haviendo llegado el Senor al monte Calvario, le desnudaron y le dieron a beber vino mezclado con hiel."

UNDECIMA ESTACION, Jesus es crucificado.

"Contempla, alma, en esta undecima estacion, como es el lugar donde fue clavado el Senor en la cruz, y oyendo su santisima Madre el primer golpe del martillo, quedo como muerta por el dolor, y le volvieron a poner la corona de espinas con gran crueldad y fiereza."

Antes del sermon se canta—"Perdón O Dios Mio."

PERDON, OH DIOS MIO

Perdón, o Dios mio
Perdón, indulgencia,
Perdón y clemencia
Perdón y piedad.

Pequé, ya mi alma
Su culpa confiesa,
Mil veces me pesa
De tanta maldad.

Mil veces me pesa
De haber mi pecado
Tu pecho rasgado,
O suma beldad.

It was I who, at the cruel
Cross, ungenerously
Placed you where you hung
With cruel impiety.

My face covered
With tears shows this,
I confess publicly
This so great truth.

For me, in torment
You shed your blood,
And captured me when I was far
From love and humility.

I have repaid you
With sin after sin,
I have filled the cup
Of wickedness.

But now, repentant,
I seek you, weeping,
O loving Father![28]
O God of goodness!

I now intend never
To betray you with treason,
O heaven, my life
Save right away.

May my humble prayer
Pierce the clouds;
May burning cherubs
Lift up my vows.

Jesus, in my heart
Rule all things:
Happy kingship—
Blessed charity!

---

28 *Any reference to Christ as "Father" suggests a likely Penitente influence.*

Yo fuí quien del duro
Madero, inclemente
Te puso pendiente
Con vil impiedad.

Mi rostro cubierto
De llanto lo indica:
Mi lengua publica
Tan triste verdad.

Por mí en tormentos
Tu sangre vertiste,
Y prenda me diste
De amor y humildad.

Yo en recompensa
Pecado a pecado
La copa he llenado
De la iniquidad.

Mas ya arrepentido
Te busco lloroso,
¡Oh Padre amoroso!
¡Oh Dios de bondad!

No intento ya nunca
Traición fementida:
¡Oh cielos mi vida
Primero quitad!

Mi humilde plegaria
Traspase las nubes;
Ardientes Querubes,
Mis votos llevad.

Jesús en mi pecho
Domine imperioso:
¡Domino dichoso,
Feliz caridad!

Your love, my Jesus,
Will be my desire;
Lovers of heaven,
Praise his love.

My God, consume away
My life, this passion,
And admit me soon
To the everlasting city.

TWELFTH STATION, Jesus dies on the cross.

"Contemplate, my soul, at this twelfth station, what the place is like where the Lord has been crucified; they let his cross fall with a painful shock into the hole in the rock."

Finally, the priest reads the Gospel from the Holy Scriptures (John 19:16-37). Here the curtain is drawn aside. Jesus Christ is seen nailed to the cross. Mary Most Holy, Saint John, Joseph and Nicodemus, the soldiers, the centurion, blind Longinus[29] and the rest of the Jews stand beneath the cross. They all present a most heartrending scene, all gazing up at Jesus Christ dead on the cross.

29 The explanation for ciego–"blind"–Longino is that the centurion, a soldier, or a beggar whom the soldiers hired or forced to do a job they found unpleasant touched the blood and water from the pierced side of Christ to his eyes and was cured of blindness or of some eye ailment. The episode occurs in twelfth-century Anglo-Norman and German-Latin passion plays (see David Bevington, Medieval Drama [Boston: Houghton Mifflin, 1975], pp. 126, 222); in just about all the extant fourteenth- to sixteenth-century English cycle plays (York, N-Town [Coventry], Chester, Cornish Ordinalia); and in Jacobus de Voragine's Legenda Aurea—The Golden Legend (New York: Longmans, Green, 1941), p. 191.

The character Longinus seems to have originated in the fifth-century apocryphal "Acts of Pilate" and "Gospel of Nicodemus"; see E. Hennecke and W. Schneemelcher, eds., New Testament Apocrypha (London: Lutterworth Press, 1963), p. 469.

In Tomé, Longinus was understood to be a soldier of Arabic descent with eye trouble.

Tu amor, Jesús mío,
Será ya mi anhelo;
Amantes del cielo,
Su amor ensalzad.

Dios mío, consuma
Mi vida ese fuego
Y admítame luego
La eterna ciudad.

DUODECIMA ESTACION, Jesus muere en la cruz.
"Contempla, alma en esta duodecima estacion, como es el lugar donde ya crucificado el Senor, le dejaron caer de golpe en el agujero de una pena."

Al Terminar, lee en la Sagrada Escritura el Evangelio. Aqui se rompe el velo. Se descubre Jesucristo clavado en la Cruz. Maria Santisima, San Juan, Jose y Nicodemos, Los Soldados, El centurion, El ciego Longino y demas Judios estan debajo de la cruz. Todos actuan una escena muy lastimosa, todos mirando a Jesucristo muerto en la cruz.

A SERMON ON THE DEPOSITION OF CHRIST
BY THE REVEREND FATHER JOSE ASSENMACHER
THREE IN THE AFTERNOON—GOOD FRIDAY

In the name of the Father and of the Son and of the Holy Spirit, amen.

I HAVE GIVEN YOU AN EXAMPLE.

With a heavy heart we begin our considerations, and with the grace of our Lord we can turn to meditation on the drama of the crucifixion of Our Lord.

Crucified! What sorrow! What does this statement mean? Moses, a thousand years before the passion of Our Lord, said that "The dead one was crucified, hanged upon the tree!" Now we should consider these few words:

"On the tree he was defeated and saved at the same time."

I mean this tree, the dividing line between good and evil, the tree of salvation or the tree of condemnation. A new Adam was needed to cleanse and save mankind.

To achieve this, the tree had to be cut on some high hill. His hands and feet had to be nailed to this cross. What terrible agonies! He spoke seven words, while the crowd taunted him as he hung between two thieves, one cursing him and the other converted by God's great favor.

There is one word which cannot well be understood:

"My God, my God, why have you forsaken me?"

Our Lord speaks the first verse of the Twenty-first Psalm of the hundred and fifty hymns of King David, one of the most poignant addresses to God. "Why have you abandoned me? You have never abandoned me—I know that you have not."

"The fierce mob surrounds me. I am dealt with like a worm. My clothing is sold."

We may compare the fierce mob to wild animals.

Let us then continue this psalm, the better to realize those sufferings. "They have pierced my feet and my hands with terrible nails."

His hands which blessed the children, the blind, and the sick. His feet which walked among the people to bring about his welcome visitation. He whom we first met in our baptism is now hanged upon the this cross. A foolishness! He gave us this example so that we might follow it. He had his enemies, but as for taking revenge, he did not.

He said to the holy women, "Weep not for me, weep for your sins and those of your sons which will fall upon

SERMON DEL DECENDIMIENTO
POR EL REVERENDO PADRE JOSE ASSENMACHER
TIEMPO—VIERNES SANTO A LAS 3:00 DE LA TARDE

En el nombre del Padre y del Hijo y del Espiritu Santo Amen.

EJEMPLO OS HE DADO.

Bajo este moto hemos empesado nuestras meditaciones, y con la gracia de nuestro Senor podemos volver a meditar en este drama de la crucificacion de Nuestro Senor.

Crucificado esta! Que dolor! Que significa esta palabra? Ya Moises sabia mil anos antes de la pasion de Nuestro Senor. "Muerto fue crucificado, esta pendiente en el leño!" Asi debemos considerar estas pocos palabras.

"En el leño fue vencido y salvado tambien."

Quiere decir este leño, distincion entre el bien y el mal. El leño de la salvacion o el leño de la maldicion. Se necesitaba un nuevo Adan para resanar y salvar al hombre.

Por eso hemos cortado en la alta mura este leño. Fueron clavados en esta cruz sus pies y manos. Terribles tormentos! Pasaron siete palabras, Plebe burlandolo, y entre dos ladrones, uno maldiciendolo, y el otro convertido estuvo con Dios en la aventuranza.

Una otra palabra que no esta bien entendida:

"Dios mio, Dios mio, porque me has abandonado?" Nuestro Senor empezo el salmo 21 de las 150 canticos del Rey David, el cual es uno de los mas salientes en Dios. "Porque me has abandonado? Siempre no me has abandonado, yo se que no."

"Alrrededor esta la gente feroz. Soy tratado como un gusano. Mis vestidos son vendidos."

Podemos comparar la gente como animales feroces.

Asi voy a continuar este salmo, paro mejor realizar estos tormentos. "Traspasados mis pies y manos con clavos terribles!"

Sus manos que bendiciendo a los ninos, los ciegos y enfermos. Sus pies caminando entre la gente para alcanzar la bien-aventuranza. Lo que hemos alcansado por el bautismo, y ahora colgado en esta cruz. Una locura! El dio el ejemplo para que nosotros lo sigamos. El tuvo sus enemigos pero tomar venganza, no.

Dijo a las Senoras piadosas, "No lloren por mi, lloren por sus culpas y las de sus hijos que van a caer sobre Jerusalen."

EL DESCENDIMIENTO

Jerusalem."

This tree is the memorial to remind us that we should forgive. If he forgave, so you should forgive if you want to be a brother to Christ. He was condemned with Dismas and Gestas; he was crucified right between them.

"I thirst."

He was thirsty! Greater torments. And another word, "In your hands am I, oh Lord! In peace with you I wish to depart this world." This was the tree of condemnation for the Jews.

This cross! The world changes, but the cross remains. All things will pass away, but without the cross there is no salvation. If the cross is our condemnation, we will be punished for everything. But if it is our hope we should imitate Our Savior and carry it.

And of this cross, it does not matter what the world says of it. Jesus Christ with his cross is victorious. He rose a short time after. This is the cross. We find it on our rosaries, in our homes, on our churches and our graves, and all the while we can find nothing to equal the cross.

Christ suffered so very much for my salvation. Let us listen to Holy Scripture the better to appreciate the death of Our Lord, dying on the cross for our salvation.

In the name of the Father and of the Son and of the Holy Spirit, amen.

Here are prayed the last two stations of the Way of the Cross.

Here blind Longinus pierces Christ's side with a lance.

THIRTEENTH STATION, The virgin receives and adores the body of her most holy son.

"Contemplate, my soul, in this thirteenth station, what the place is like where Joseph and Nicodemus lower the holy body from the cross and place it in the arms of the Most Holy Virgin."

Now Joseph and Nicodemus lower the body from the cross. Joseph ascends the ladder and frees the body, Nicodemus takes it in his arms and presents it to the Most Holy Virgin. Then they lay him on a shroud. Two women with a pitcher of water wash the blood from his face and body and then place the body in a coffin after it has been embalmed.

The lining of the coffin is silk. The coffin is covered with fresh flowers. After he is placed in the coffin the people sprinkle perfume on him.

Este leño es senal para recordar que debemos perdonar. Si El perdono, asi tu perdona si debes de ser hermano en Cristo. Estubo culpado como Dimas y Gestas. Fue crucificado en medio de ellos.

"Tengo sed!"

Tenia sed! Mas Tormentos. Y otra palabra, "En tus manos estoy Senor! En tu paz quiero salir de este mundo." Aqui esta el leño de la maldicion de los Judios.

Esta Cruz! El mundo esta rodando, pero la cruz esta firme. Todo debe pasar pero sin cruz no hay salvacion. Si es la cruz una maldicion todos debemos pagar. O si es nuestra esperanza debemos imitar a Nuestro Salvador y llevarla.

La cruz esta, no importa que el mundo diga. Jesucristo con su cruz esta triunfando. El resucito mas tarde. Aqui esta la cruz. La vemos en nuestros rosarios, en nuestros hogares, en las iglesias y en nuestras tumbas y mientras la vemos nada en comparacion de la cruz.

El padecio asi terrible por mi salvacion. Sigamos la Sagrada Escritura para mejor apreciar la muerte de Nuestro Senor en la cruz por nuestra redencion.

En el nombre del Padre y del Hijo y del Espirito Santo Amen.

Aqui se resan las dos ultimas estaciones del Via Crucis.

Aqui el ciego Longino Atrevisa su santo costado con una lanza.

DECIMATERCIA ESTACION, La virgen resibe y adora el cuerpo de su santisimo hijo.

"Contempla, alma, en esta decimatertia estacion, como es el lugar donde Jose y Nicodemos bajaron el santo cuerpo de la cruz, y lo pusieron en los brazos de la Santisima Virgen."

Aqui Jose y Nicodemus lo abajan de la cruz. Jose se sube por la escalera y lo desata, Nicodemos lo toma en sus brazos y se lo presenta a la Santisima Virgen. Despues lo echan en una sabana. Dos senoras con un pichel de agua le limpian la sangre del rostro y el cuerpo y despues es puesto en la urna despues de haber sido enbalsamado.

La cama en la urna es de seda. La urna esta cubierta de frores frescas. Despues de ser puesto en la urna la gente le echan perfume.

FOURTEENTH STATION, The body of Jesus is laid in the tomb.

"Comtemplate, my soul, what the place is like where the Virgin Mary, Our Lady, lays the body of her beloved Son in the holy sepulchre."

The procession goes forward.

"AMANTE JESUS MIO"[30]

Whoever looks on your dead body
Hanging on the cross
Sees the sacrifice for our sins,
Sees you die, Holy Jesus.
   My Jesus full of love,
   O how often I have offended you!
   Forgive my transgressions
   And have mercy on me.[31]
In your compassion and pity,
Not liable to punishment for sin
You have I wounded
With hateful ingratitude.

You who gave sight to the blind man
And gave speech to the mute
And new life could
Give to Lazarus,
Are hanged today on the cross
And dying among insults
Of the fickle crowd,
You who came to redeem them.

---

30 As the procession is being formed and as it sets out, the following hymn is sung.

31 These four lines make up a kind of chorus, but in subsequent stanzas, instead of these lines being repeated, the second half of the stanza is sung to the tune of "My Jesus, full of love . . . have mercy on me.

DECIMACUARTA ESTACION, Es colocado en el sepulcro el cuerpo de Jesus.

"Contempla, alma, en esta ultima estacion, como es el lugar donde la Virgen Maria, Senora nuestra, puso el cuerpo de su querido Hijo en el santo sepulcro."

Sale la procesion.

"AMANTE JESUS MIO"

Quien al mirarte exanime
Pendiente de una cruz,
Por nuestras culpas victima
Expirar buen Jesús.
  Amante Jesús mío,
  O cuanto te ofendi!
  Perdona mi estravio
  Y ten piedad de mi.
De compasión y lastima
No siente el pecho herido
Habiendo te ofendido
Con negra ingratitud.

Quien dió la vista al ciego,
quien dió la voz al mudo,
Quien nueva vida pudo
A Lázaro infundir,
Hoy pende de un madero,
Y expira escarnecido
Del pueblo fementido
Que viene a redemir.

The bedrock tore asunder,
The sky gave no light,
And there trembled, tearing the veil
The temple of the Lord;
And the Cherubim, seeing
The terrifying cross,
Fixed toward the earth
Stares of amazement.

The blood which has been shed
By the nails and the lance
Demands to be revenged,
Seeming to cry out:
Will no thunderbolt descend
To incinerate into
Its ashes, this world
Which forever rebels?

But if I die on the cross today
As a judge will appoint soon,
Coming on the clouds of fire
For whoever violatated Sinai,
O, if then I have lost
Your holy grace, I weep.
My God, I ask your mercy;
I have sinned, woe is me!

The centurion goes ahead on a white horse decked out in
mourning.
The Most Holy Cross.
Our Lady of Solitude.
Saint John
The soldiers
The Lord in the coffin.
The Jews
The Servers
The Priest

148

Quebrántase la roca,
Sin luz se queda el cielo,
Retiembla, roto el velo,
El templo del Señor.
Y, al ver los Querubines
La Crus que los aterra,
dirigen a la tierra
miradas de estupor.

La sangre que han vertido
los clavos y la lanza
pidiendo estan venganza;
parecen exclamar:
¿No descenderá el rayo
para hacer furibundo
cenizas ese mundo
rebelde sin cesar?

Pero, si en Cruz hoy muere,
como juez vendrá luego,
sobre nubes de fuego,
cual vióle el Sinaí.
Ay! si entonces perdida
tu santa gracia lloro!
Mi Dios! Piedad imploro.
Pequé. Triste de mi!

El Centurion va adelante en un caballo blanco cubierto de luto
La Santisima cruz
Nuestra Senora de la Soledad.
San Juan
Los Soldados
El Senor En La Urna.
Los Judios
Los Sacristanes
Los Sacerdote

EL CENTURION

TOME
8/11/47

NUESTRO SENOR EN LA URNA

The Choir, who sing "Miserere Mei Deus."[32]

During the procession there are five stops made, representing the five wounds of Our Lord. The table for setting the coffin down is draped in mourning. There are five incensations. At the end of the procession the priest gives his blessing.

GOOD FRIDAY   APRIL 19, 1946

SCENE FOUR

THE SERMON ON OUR LADY OF SOLITUDE

PERSONAGES

The Priest
The Servers
The Jews   (The same as in previous acts.)
The Soldiers
The Choir ....they sing "Venid Almas Devotas,"
"Ayudemos Almas," and "Stabat Mater."

The Holy Body in the coffin ....carried by:
Miguel Salazar, Fred Landavazo,
Francisco Baca, Tobias Lucero,
Ventura Sanchez, Pat Sanchez

Our Lady of Solitude ....carried by:
Mrs. Toribio Chavez, Mrs. Cosme Sanchez

Saint John ....carried by: Seferino Sanchez,
Nicanor Sanchez

Three children ....(The same as before; they carry
the crown of thorns, a nail, the hammer)

The Most Holy Cross ....carried by: Crestino Baca

---

32 The text of "Miserere Mei Deus" appears above.

El Coro canta "Miserere Mei Deus"

Durante la procesion hay cinco paradas, representando las cinco llagas de nuestro Senor. La mesa para descansar el cuerpo va de luto. Se ofrece incensio cinco veces. Terminada la procesion el sacerdote echa la bendicion.

VIERNES SANTO   ABRIL 19, 1946

ESCENA CUARTA

EL SERMON DE LA SOLEDAD

PERSONAJES

El Sacerdote
Los Sacristanes
Los Judios   (Los Mismos de los actos anteriores.)
Los Soldados

El Coro ....se canta "Venid Almas Devotas,"
                        "Ayudemos Almas," y "Stabat Mater."

El Santo Entierro en la urna ....Llevado por:
                        Miguel Salazar, Fred Landavazo,
                        Francisco Baca, Tobias Lucero,
                        Ventura Sanchez, Pat Sanchez

Nuestra Senora de la Soledad ....Llevada por:
                        Sra. Toribio Chavez, Sra. Cosme Sanchez

San Juan ....Llevado por: Seferino Sanchez,
                        Nicanor Sanchez

Tres ninos ....(Los mismos de la tarde y llevan:
                        la corona, un clavo, el martillo)

La Santisima cruz ....Llevada por: Crestino Baca

THE SERMON ON OUR LADY OF SOLITUDE

The action takes place at the main altar and during the procession around the plaza.

It begins at seven in the evening.

Our Lord Jesus Christ lying in the coffin.

Our Lady of Solitude and Saint John stand at his side.

The Jews keep vigil and say their rosaries.

The priest and servers enter, and he delivers the sermon of Our Lady of Solitude.

"VENID ALMAS DEVOTAS"

Come, devout souls,
Come, come, come,
And the most sorrowful Mother
Join in mourning;
"Woe is me, woe is me!
What crime did my Son commit
To die this way?"

At the foot of a rough tree
I saw a turtledove
Who, sad and afflicted,
Mourned in these words:
"Woe is me, woe is me!"
What crime did my Son commit
To die this way?

"My God and my Lord
Has died and I look on;
And not like one of the living
Is he since I lost him.
Woe is me, woe is me!
I who before was so happy
Am miserable now.

EL SERMON DE LA SOLEDAD

El escenario toma lugar en el altar mayor de despues la procesion por la plaza.

Tiempo a la 7:00 de la tarde.

Nuestro Senor Jesucristo esta tendido en la urna.

Nuestra Senora de la Soledad y San Juan estan a su lado.

Los Judios lo velan y rretocan los rosarios.

Entran el Sacerdote y los sacristanes, sigue el sermon de la Soledad.

VENID, ALMAS DEVOTAS

Venid, almas devotas,
Venid, venid, venid;
Y a la más triste Madre
Ayudadia a sentir.
¡Ay de mí, mas ay de mí!
¿Qué culpa tuvo mi Hijo
Para morir así.

Al pie de un tosco leño
Una tórtola vi,
Que triste y afligida
Se lamentaba así:
¡Ay de mí, mas ay de mí!
¿Qué culpa tuvo mi Hijo
Para morir así.

"Mi Dios y mi Señor
Ha muerto y yo lo vi;
Y no sé cómo vivo
Después que le perdí.
¡Ay de mí, mas ay de mí!
Que siendo antes dichosa
Ahora soy infeliz.

NUESTRA SEÑORA DE LA SOLEDAD

"If my Life is dead
Why do I not die?
If my Jesus is no more
What do I have to live for?
Woe is me, woe is me!
If he had to suffer
Why did I give him birth?

I bore him because I chose to
And because I knew
That God's holy will
Determined it so.
Woe is me, woe is me!
May it be your will, sweet Jesus,
That I die for you.

"Jesus of my soul,
If I was your Mother
Why do you leave me lonely?
What is the reason, pray?
Woe is me, woe is me!
That I no longer find the blossoms
That were in my garden yesterday.

"The rose has withered,
The jasmine faded away;
My carnation, my lily
On the cross have died.
Woe is me, woe is me!
Their perfumes are gone.
I cannot go further.

"Hearken, attend,
Children beloved,
To the lamentations
Of this my great woe.
Woe is me, woe is me!
Alone, without my Jesus,
I cannot live on.

"Si mí Vida murió,
¿Por qué no yo morí,
Si mí Jesús se fué,
¿Qué hago yo aquí?
¡Ay de mí, mas hay de mí!
Si había de padecer,
¿Por qué yo le parí?

"Lo parí porque quise
Y porque conocí
Que El de su voluntad
Lo determinó así.
¡Ay de mí, mas ay de mí!
Haz, oh dulce Jesús,
Que muera yo por tí.

"Jesús del alma mía
Si yo tu Madre fuí,
¿Por qué me dejas sola?
¿Cuál es la causa, dí?
¡Ay de mí, mas ay de mí!
Que no encuentro las flores
De mi antiguo jardín.

"Se ha secado la rosa,
Se marchitó el jazmín;
Mi clavel, mi azucena
En la cruz dieron fin.
¡Ay de mí, mas ay de mí!
Faltando sus olores.
No les puedo seguir.

"Escuchad atentos,
Hijos de mi amor,
Las lamentaciones
De este mi gran dolor.
¡Ay de mí, mas ay de mí!
Sola y sin mi Jesús,
Yo no puedo vivir.

"My Jesus has died,
My Son is gone away,
God my very life
Has left and abandoned me.
Woe is me, woe is me!
Alone, without my Jesus,
I cannot live on.

"Alone and without comfort
I cry to my Son
Since my sweet delight
Has left and abandoned me.
Woe is me, woe is me!
Alone, without my Jesus,
I cannot live on.

"Attend to my pain,
Behold my affliction;
Since my beloved
Has left and abandoned me.
Woe is me, woe is me!
Alone, without my Jesus,
I cannot live on.

"But I console myself
By standing with you
Who henceforth are my children
Born of my heart.
Woe is me, woe is me!
Without Jesus, only by you,
My children, can I live on."

"Mi Jesús ha muerto,
Mi Hijo se ausentó,
El Dios de mi vida
Se fué y me dejó.
¡Ay de mí, mas ay de mí!
Sola y sin mi Jesús,
Yo no puedo vivir.

"Sola y sin consuelo
Lloro a mi Señor,
Pues mi dulce encanto
Se fué y me dejó.
¡Ay de mí, mas ay de mí!
Sola y sin mi Jesús,
Yo no puedo vivir.

"Atended a mi pena,
Mirad mi aflicción;
Pues que mi afición,
Se fué y me dejó.
¡Ay de mí, mas ay de mí!
Sola y sin mi Jesús,
Yo no puedo vivir.

"Pero me consuelo
Con estar con vos,
Que también, sois mis hijos
De mi corazón.
¡Ay de mí, mas ay de mí!
Sin Jesús sólo por vos,
Hijos, puedo vivir."

A SERMON ON OUR LADY OF SOLITUDE
BY THE REVEREND FATHER JOSE ASSENMACHER
SEVEN IN THE EVENING—GOOD FRIDAY

In the name of the Father and of the Son and of the Holy Spirit, amen.

I HAVE GIVEN YOU AN EXAMPLE.

With downcast hearts, we have been meditating this year on the words and teachings of the passion of Our Lord, so as to achieve a heart properly repentant and to attain eternal life. This sermon we consecrate to Our Sorrowful Mother. We weep from our birth to our death, for we live in an ocean of tears. The disciple is not better than his master.

Mary Most Holy knew very well that a sword would pierce her heart. Here we recall Mary Most Holy three and thirty years before, when the Angel Gabriel announced to her the coming of the Savior. That started the whole process, that mere word, and it continued for thirty-three years.

Most Holy Mary, in her solitude, saw in a vision Our Lord in Gethsemani—alone, sweating tears of blood, his disciples asleep. Most Holy Mary alone chose to stand beneath the cross of her son. Years past a mother had held her little baby and fed him at her breast; and now he was suffering. Great as the ocean was her sorrow. What can explain this sorrow of Mary Most Holy? To know, we must have devotion to this Sorrowful Mother. Her love was greater than that of mother for son; by contrast, it was a love of a mother for her God.

The years passed between the nativity and the death, and always we see a mother who loves her son. They flee into Egypt, they seek him when he is lost in the temple. What sorrow!

When Jesus began his public life, what eagerness the Mother had whenever he returned to her or when she received word of him. She knew very well, for he had revealed it, that he was going to be crucified to redeem the world. As the years passed, the passion drew near. She knew that he was going to die, that a friend would be his betrayer. In the night when he was in his agony she suffered as well. She knew that he was going to be condemned because Saint John brought her the news. She followed him toward Mount Calvary; she saw him when they placed the cross on his shoulders. At the Fourth Station of the Way of the Cross she met him, just as we have considered it before.

The Sorrowful Mother stood beneath the cross not like a

SERMON DE NUESTRA SENORA DE LA SOLEDAD
POR EL REVERENDO PADRE JOSE ASSENMACHER
TIEMPO—VIERNES SANTO A LAS 7:00 DE LA NOCHE

En el nombre del Padre y del Hijo y del Espiritu Santo Amen.

EJEMPLO OS HE DADO.

Bajo este moto, palabra y doctrina hemos este ano meditado la pasion de Nuestro Senor. Para tener un corazon bien arrepentido y para llevar una vida eterna. Estas palabras dedicamos a Nuestra Madre Dolorosa. Lagrimas desde la cuna hasta la muerte, porque vivemos en un mar de lagrimas. El dicipulo no es mayor que su maestro.

Maria Santisima supo muy bien que una espada iba a traspasar su corazon. Aqui teniamos a Maria Santisima treinta y tres anos antes, el Angel Gabriel anunciando la venida del Salvador. Ella actuo, sola una palabra, y duro treinta y tres anos.

Maria Santisima en su Soledad, vio a Nuestro Senor en Jesemani solo sudando lagrimas de sangre, sus amigos dormidos. Maria Santisima sola debajo la cruz con su hijo querido. Anos pasados una madre tenia su bebito. Con sus pechos le alimentaba. Pero ahora sufriendo. Grande como el mar era su dolor. Quien puede explicar el dolor de Maria Santisima? Por eso debemos esta devocion a esta Madre Dolorosa. Era Amor mas grande que Madre e hijo. En comparacion era un Dios y una Madre.

Anos recorrieron desde el nacimiento hasta su muerte, y siempre vemos una Madre que ama a su nino. Huyeron a Ejipto, perdido en el templo. Que Mas dolor!

Cuando Jesus empeso su vida publica que ancias tenia esta Madre cuando El volvia o cuando recebia noticias de El. Ella supo muy bien y le fue revelado que el iba a ser crucificado por redemir al mundo. Cuando pasaron los anos llego su pasion. Ella supo que iba a morir, que un amigo iba a ser su traidor. En la noche que el sufrio tambien ella sufrio. Ella supo cuando iban a condenar a Jesus porque San Juan el llevo la noticia. Ella lo sigio al Monte Calvario. Vio cuando le cargaron la cruz. En la cuarta estacion del via cruces lo encontro, conforme hemos meditado.

Estaba Maria Dolorosa, no como un cuadro, estaba fuerte,

statue, without fainting, standing strong, knowing how to bear her sorrow. In her anguish she wept pearls from her heart. And finally they placed his body in her arms at the foot of the cross.

Who of us knows the councils of God? Does anyone love his children as Mary Most Holy loved Jesus? Why can we not? We know already that at birth we contract an illness from which we will die; why can we not resign ourselves to it?

Mary Most Holy had to suffer as did Our Lord. If he had not undergone his passion, we would not have received salvation.

God bless thee, Sorrowful Mother, full of tears!

The Lord was with thee all thy life, and blessed art thou above all other women.

Holy Mary, full of sorrows, pray for us.

Jesus has died on the cross, but the love of the mother goes on to endure more. Like the love of the mother is the love of the son for us. On Gethsemani he had called out to his Heavenly Father, "Father, let your highest will be done!"

That was the heart that died on Mount Calvary so that we might have eternal life.

From the cross to the light!

Through the passion to salvation and Christian fortitude!

In the name of the Father and of the Son and of the Holy Spirit, amen.

* * *

After the sermon there is a procession around the plaza.

Order of the procession
The Cross
The servers
Our Lady of Solitude
Saint John
The soldiers
The Holy Body in the coffin
The three children
The Jews
The priest
The choir—they sing "Stabat Mater Dolorosa" and "Ayudemos Almas."

supo soportar el dolor. Afligida llorando perlas de su corazon. Al fin al pie de la cruz lo pusieron en sus brazos.

Quien de nosotros sabe las consejos de Dios? Si uno amara a sus hijos como Maria Santisima amo a Jesus! Porque nosotros no podemos? Ya sabemos que desde el nacimiento tenemos esta infeccion de que vamos a morir. Porque no nos resignamos?

Maria Santisima fue obligada a sufrir como Nuestro Senor. Si El no ubiera sufrido su pasion, no tuvieramos redencion.

Dios te salve Maria Dolorosa llena de lagrimas interiores! El Senor estuvo con tigo toda tu vida, y bendita tu eres entre todas las mujeres. Santa Maria de los dolores ruega por nosotros.[33]

Jesus murio en la cruz pero el amor de la madre va a durar mas. Como el amor de la madre asi el del hijo para nosotros. En Jesemani aclamando a su Padre Celestial. Padre sera tu suma voluntad!

Un corazon como ella paso al Monte Calvario para que tengamos gloria eterna.

Por la cruz a la luz!

Por la pasion a la salvacion y a la fortaleza!

En el nombre del Padre y del Hijo y del Espititu Santo Amen.

* * *

Despues del sermon sigue la procesion por la plaza.

Orden de la procesion
La Crus
Los Sacristanes
Nuestra Senora de la Soledad
San Juan
Los Soldados
El Santo Entierro en la urna
Tres ninos
Los Judios
El Sacerdote
El coro—se canta "Stabat Mater Dolorosa" y "Ayudemos Almas"

---

33 *These three sentences are a revision of the hymn "Dios Te Salve" which appears as part of the Easter material; it is a version of the familiar Catholic Hail Mary.*

"ESTABAS, MADRE DOLOROSA"[34]

At the Cross her station keeping,
Stood the mournful Mother weeping,
Close to Jesus to the last.

Through her heart, His sorrow sharing,
All His bitter anguish bearing,
Lo! the piercing sword had passed.

O how sad and sore distressed
Was that Mother, highly blessed,
Of the sole-begotten One.

Woe-begone, with heart's prostration,
Mother meek, the bitter passion
Saw she of her glorious Son.

Who on Christ's dear Mother gazing,
In her trouble so amazing,
Born of woman, would not weep?

Who on Christ's dear Mother thinking,
Such a cup of sorrow drinking,
Would not share her sorrow deep?

For His people's sins rejected,
Saw her Jesus unprotected,
Saw with thorns, with scourges rent:

Saw her Son from judgment taken
Her Beloved in death forsaken,
Till His spirit forth He sent.

Fount of love and holy sorrow;
Mother! may my spirit borrow
Somewhat of thy woe profound;

---

34 *This is the standard English translation of the medieval Latin hymn* Stabat
Mater, *traditionally but doubtfully attributed to the Franciscan Jacopone da
Todi (c.1230-c.1306). Both the Spanish and the English are loose translations
of the original, but all versions are very decidedly in the mainline tradition of
early Franciscan spirituality.*

ESTABAS, MADRE DOLOROSA

Estabas, Madre dolorosa,
Al pie de la cruz llorosa
Donde pende el Redentor.

Cuyo espíritu paciente
Traspasaba vivamente
Una espada de dolor.

¡Oh, qué triste y afligida
Fuiste, Reina esclarecida,
Virgen y Madre de Dios!

¡Qué dolores! ¡Qué agonías!
Cuando tú las penas veías
Del Hijo más ínclito!

¿Quién será aquél que no llora
Contemplando a esta Señora,
En tan grande suplicio?

¿Quién no puede enternecerse,
Viendo a esta Madre dolerse
Con su Unigénito?

Vió por los pecadores
Fué oprimido de dolores,
Y azotado sin piedad.

Vió a Jesús la triste Madre,
Desamparado del Padre,
Entregar su espíritu.

Fuente del amor, María,
Haz sienta en tu compañía
Un dolor vivísimo.

Unto Christ, with pure emotion,
Raise my contrite heart's devotion,
Love to read in every wound.

Those five wounds on Jesus smitten,
Mother! in my heart be written,
Deep as in thine own they be;

Thou, thy Saviour's Cross who bearest,
Thou, thy Son's rebuke who sharest,
Let me share them both with thee.

In the passion of my Maker,
Be my sinful soul partaker,
Weep till death and weep with thee;

Mine with thee be that sad station,
There to watch the great salvation,
Wrought upon the atoning tree.

Virgin, thou of virgins farest,
May the bitter woe thou bearest,
Make on me impression deep.

Thus Christ's dying may I carry,
With Him in His passion tarry,
And His wounds in memory keep.

May His wound both wound and heal me,
He enkindle, cleanse, anneal me,
Be His Cross my hope and stay.

May He, when the mountains quiver,
From that flame which burns for ever,
Shield me on the judgment day.

Jesus, may Thy Cross defend me,
And Thy Mother's prayer befriend me,
Let me die in Thy embrace;

When to dust my dust returneth,
Grant a soul that to Thee yearneth.
In Thy Paradise a place. Amen.

Haz que fiel y enamorado,
Sirva siempre con agrado
A tu Hijo y mi Señor.

Santa Madre, aquesto hagas
Del Crucifijo las llagas
Grabes en mi corazón.

Pues por mí padece tanto,
Hoy conmigo este quebranto
De sus penas dividid.

Haz, Señora, que a tu lado,
Llore yo al crucificado,
Sin cesar hasta morir.

Al pie de la Cruz deseo
Imitar el dulce empleo
De tu llanto y compasión.

No me niegues, Virgen pura,
Que contigo la amargura
De este cáliz beba yo.

Haz que su pasión imite,
Que en sus penas me ejercite
Y en su muerte con fervor.

De sus llagas vulnerdo,
Y de su cruz embriagado,
Y de tu sangre también.

Del infierno y sus horrores
Libranos por tus dolores,
En el día del juicio.

Buen Jesús, luego me muera
Por tu amante Madre espera
Salvarse este pecador.

En la hora de mi muerte
Haz que logre yo la suerte
De tu eterna bendición.

"AYUDEMOS, ALMAS"

Let us help, oh souls,
In the great sorrow
Of the pure Virgin
Of Solitude.[35]

At the foot of the cross
Her we see who is
Mother bereft of Son
For he is now dead.

How it increases her anguish
To look at Jesus.
There is no one to take him down
From the holy cross.

Her sorrow swells
Since she has no shroud
To clothe again
His holy body.

So poor is she
That she owns no tomb
To bury the body
Of her departed Son.

Three great needs
Our lady had,
But God sent those
Who will come to her aid.

---

35 Nuestra Señora de la Soledád is a title of Our Lady as the woman
bereft of husband and children, the crone; she is patroness of lonely women
who have lost their families. It was imagined that after the death of Christ (and
even after the resurrection) she lived a nunlike life, so she is usually shown in
nunlike garb.

AYUDEMOS ALMAS

Ayudemos, almas,
De tanto penar
A la Virgen pura
De la Soledad.

Al pie de la cruz,
La vemos que está
La Madre sin Hijo,
Porque ha muerto ya.

Se aumenta su pena
De ver a Jesús.
Que no hay quien lo baje
De la santa cruz.

Crece su dolor,
Pues no halla sudario
Para revestir
El cuerpo sagrado.

Tanta es su pobreza,
Pues no hay un sepulcro
Para sepultar el cuerpo
De su Hijo difunto.

Tres necesidades
Tuvo esta Señora:
Pero Dios le envía
Quien se las socorra.

Nicodemus and Joseph
Of Arimathea[36]
Lower the body
And give it to Mary.

In her holy arms
Tenderly she holds it;
With bitter tears
She kissed the wounds.

"O Son of my soul,
Let me die with you!
See how your body is
All become one wound!

"For the sins of others
He came to this end,
To free mankind
From eternal death."

The sepulchre of Jesus
Caused his Mother
Such pain and sorrow
Her heart was broken.

With Saint John she went
For he was the beloved
To whom Jesus
Had entrusted her.

There she saw the street
Where they had taken him,
And where the fatal
Sentence was given.

Sad and sorrowful
She entered the city
Full of sorrow,
Full of sadness.

36 The Spanish text mislocates the epithet "De Arimatea," giving it to
Nicodemus. It could be that both men were popularly understood to have
been from the same town, for the text as given by the Oblates of Mary
Immaculate in Canticos Mexicanos (San Antonio: Mazenod, 1933), p. 30,
shows the same irregularity.

José y Nicodemo
De Arimatea
Bajan a Jesús,
Y a María lo entregan.

En sus dulces brazos
Tierna lo estrechaba,
Con amargo llanto
Sus llagas besaba.

Ay Hijo de mi alma,
Prenda de mi vida,
¡Cómo está tu cuerpo
Todo hecho una herida!

Por culpas ajenas
Está de esta suerte:
Por librar al hombre
De la eterna muerte.

Sepulcro a Jesús
Dieron, a su Madre
De pena y de dolor
El pecho se le abre.

Con San Juan se va,
Porque es el amado,
A quien Jesucristo
La había encomendado.

Allí vió la calle
Donde le prendieron,
Y donde de muerte
Sentencia le dieron.

Triste y afligida,
Entra en la ciudad
Llena de dolor,
Llena de pesar.

Entering her house
She gave way to tears;
There was no one to comfort her
In such an affliction.

You, man, were the cause
Of that solitude,
Weeping your sin,
Weeping your evil.

Wounding your heart
With seven swords;
Your eyes with crying,
Lady, you weep away.

"Where is my beloved?"
She says, in sorrow.
"Where is my good,
Where is my life?"

Hail, sorrowful,
Afflicted Mother,
Hail, for your sorrows
Bring salvation to us all.

Farewell, my Mother,
Farewell, my consolation,
Farewell, my hope,
Farewell, my help.

*   *   *

After the procession the priest gives his blessing.

Entra en su aposento
Se desata en llanto;
No hay quien la consuele
En tanto quebranto.

Hombre, fuiste causa
De esta soledad:
Llora tu pecado,
Llora tu maldad.

Herido tu pecho
Con siete puñales,
Tus ojos en llanto,
Señora, deshaces.

¿Dónde está mi amado?
Decía dolorida.
¿Dónde está mi bien,
Dónde está mi vida?

Salve, dolorosa,
Afligida Madre,
Salve, tus dolores
A todos nos salven.

Adiós, Madre mía,
Adiós, mi consuelo,
Adiós, mi esperanza,
Adiós, mi remedio.

*   *   *

Terminada la procesion el sacerdote echa la vendicion.

HOLY SATURDAY   APRIL 20, 1946

ACT FOUR

The ceremonies begin at seven in the morning.
The [blessing of the] fire
The blessing of the Pascal candle.
The blessing of the [baptismal] water.
The readings.[37]
Holy Mass.

PERSONAGES

The priest

The servers . . . . .The same as in previous acts.

The Holy Body . . . . .carried by: Miguel Salazar,
Juan Estevan Zamora, Pat Sanchez,
Trinidád Romero, Nicanor Sanchez,
Seferino Sanchez

The action takes place within the church at the main altar.
This is at nine in the morning.
The priest and servers enter.
The Mass begins.
When the priest sings "Gloria in Excelsis Deo," the men who stand by the Holy Body carry it out immediately into the side chapel.
The Mass continues.

Notes and explanations: "Lumen Christi." Three candles. Five grains [of incense] in the candle, representing the incensations.[38]

---

37 The readings referred to are twelve prophecies from the Old Testament; they usually come between the candle and water ceremonies.

38 The original hand written note is dim. "Lumen Christi" are key words in the light ceremony; the three candles ("Tres velas") are part of this ceremony. The five grains are put into the Pascal candle in the form of the cross, and may have reminded the author of the note of the five incensations. See Ellis, "Passion Play," p. 211.

SABADO DE GLORIA   ABRIL 20, 1946

ACTO CUARTO

Los Oficios a las 7:00 de la manana
La Lumbre
La bendicion de la vela de Pascua.
La bendicion del agua.
Las lecturas.
La Santa Misa.

PERSONAJES

El Sacerdote
Los sacristanes . . . . .Los mismos de los actos anteriores.

El Santo Entierro . . . . .Llevado por: Miguel Salazar,
Juan Estevan Zamora, Pat Sanchez,
Trenidad Romero, Nicanor Sanchez,
Seferino Sanchez

El escenario toma lugar adentro de la iglesia delante del altar mayor.
Tiempo a la 9:00 de la manana.
Entran el Sacerdote y los sacristanes.
Comienza la Misa.
Cuando el sacerdote canta "Gloria en Excelso Deo," los hombres que estan con el Santo Entierro lo sacan prestamente para la capillita.
Sigue la Misa.

Notas y explicaciones: Lumen Christi, Tres velas, Cinco granas en el cerio Representando el incienso.

EASTER SUNDAY   APRIL 21, 1946

ACT FIVE

THE PROCESSION OF THE RESURRECTION

PERSONAGES

The priest ....Rev. Fr. José Assenmacher

The servers ....Doroteo Baca, Olmedo Baca,
David Sanchez, Hermenes Baca,
Meliton Sanchez, Tony Sanchez,
Hermenes Sanchez

Jesus Christ—(Risen)[39] ....carried by: Tobias Lucero,
José Orona, Meliton Torrez,
Fred Landavazo

Saint John ....carried by: Seferino Sanchez,
Nicanor Sanchez

The Most Holy Virgin ....carried by: Mrs. Guillie Silva,
Mrs. Esmael Sanchez, Mrs. Santiago Marquez,
Mrs. Toribio Chavez

Two men directing the procession ....Adelino Sanchez
for the men. Elauterio Sanchez for the women.

The choir which sings ...."O Filii et Filiae."

---

39 *There is another head which is affixed to the newer statue to convert it into the Risen Christ.*

DOMINGO DE RESURRECION   ABRIL 21, 1946

ACTO QUINTO

LA PROCESION DE LA RESURRECION

PERSONAJES

El Sacerdote ....Rev. Padre Jose Assenmacher

Los sacristanes ....Doroteo Baca, Olmedo Baca,
David Sanchez, Hermenes Baca,
Meliton Sanchez, Tony Sanchez,
Hermenes Sanchez

Jesucristo—(Resucitado) ....Llevado por: Tobias Lucero,
Jose Orona, Meliton Torrez,
Fred Landavazo

San Juan ....Llevado por: Seferino Sanchez,
Nicanor Sanchez

La Santisima Virgen ....Llevada por: Mrs. Guillie Silva,
Mrs. Esmael Sanchez, Mrs. Santiago Marquez,
Mrs. Toribio Chavez

Dos Hombres dirigiendo la Procesion ....Adelino Sanchez
la de los hombres. Elauterio Sanchez la de las mujeres.

El Coro—se canta ....''O Filii et Filiae''

DOMINGO DE RESURRECCION

EASTER SUNDAY

The action takes place during the procession around the plaza.

It begins at 7:30 in the morning.

The procession begins:

The men go out through the front door and the women out the south side. The procession of the men goes in two lines single file and is under the direction of Adelino Sanchez. The procession of the women is also in two lines single file and is under the direction of Elauterio Sanchez.

The servers precede the procession of the men.

Jesus Christ follows.

A boy who carries flowers.

A girl who carries a small cushion which holds the crown of thorns.

The banner of the Society of Saint Joseph

The priest

The choir—which sings "Rex Caelestis, Rex Gloriae"

The order of the procession of the women.

Saint John goes ahead

Mary Most Holy

The banners of the various societies

Saint John goes running and meets Jesus Christ, embraces him, runs to where Mary Most Holy is approaching, embraces her, runs the other way to where Christ is coming and then the other way to where the Virgin is coming and continues so until Jesus Christ and the Virgin meet. They embrace and the procession continues.

Jesus Christ in the lead.

The children

The Most Holy Virgin

Saint John

The banners of the societies.

The priest, the servers, and the choir

DOMINGO DE RESURRECION

El escenario toma lugar en la procesion por la plaza.

Tiempo a las 7:30 de la manana.

Sale la procesion:

Los hombres salen al frente Y las mujeres por el lado sur. La procesion de los hombres es de dos filas de a uno y va derigida por Adelino Sanchez. La procesion de las mujeres tambien es de dos filas de a una y es dirigida por Elauterio Sanchez.

Los sacristanes van adelante de la procesion de los hombres.

Sigue Jesucristo.

Un Nino que lleva flores

Una nina que lleva un cojincito en el cual van las espinas.

La Bandera de La sociedad de San Jose

El Sacerdote

El Coro—se canta "Rex Caelestis Rex Gloriae"

Orden de la procesion de las mujeres.

Va San Juan adelante

Maria Santisima

Las banderas de las sociedades

San Juan va corriendo y encuentra a Jesucristo, se abrazan, corre a donde viene Maria Santisimà, se abrazan, Corre otra vez para donde viene Jesucristo y otra vez para donde viene la virgen y asi continuá hasta que Jesucristo y la Virgen se encuentran. Se abrazan y siguen caminando.

Jesucristo adelante.

Los Ninos

La Santisima Virgen

San Juan

Lan Banderas de las sociedaded.

El Sacerdote, Los sacristanes y el coro

"REX CAELESTIS, REX GLORIAE"

Alleluia, alleluia, alleluia!

Ye sons and daughters, let us sing!
The King of Heav'n, our glorious King,
From death today rose triumphing,
Alleluia.

On this most holy day of days,
To God your hearts and voices raise,
In laud, and jubilee, and praise,
Alleluia.

So let us on this happy day,
Devout and humble as we pray,
Draw near to God due thanks to say,
Alleluia.[40]

"DIOS TE SALVE, MARIA"[42]

May God greet you, Mary,
You are full of grace,
The Lord is with you and you are blessed
Among all women
And blessed is the fruit of your womb, Jesus.
Holy Mary, Mother of God,
Pray for us sinners
Now and at the hour of our death.
May it be so, Jesus and Mary.

---

40 First two stanzas translated by John Mason Neale, 1851; third stanza by the present editor.

42 Informants state that this hymn and the one following were also sung during the Easter procession.

"REX CAELESTIS, REX GLORIAE"[41]

Alleluia, alleluia, alleluia!

O filii et filiae,
Rex caelestis, Rex gloriae,
Morte surrexit hodie,
Alleluia.

In hoc festo sanctissimo
Sit laus et jubilatio,
Benedicamus Domino,
Alleluia.

Ex quibus nos humillimas
Devotas atque debitas
Deo dicamus gratias,
Alleluia.

DIOS TE SALVE

Dios te Salve, María
Llena eres de gracia
El Señor es contigo y bendita tu eres
Entre todas la mujeres
Y bendito es el fruto de tu vientre Jesús.
Santa María, Madre de Dios
Ruega por nosotros los pecadores
Ahora y en la hora de nuestra muerte.
Así sea, Jesús Maria.

---

41 By Jean Tisserant, d. 1494.

"EL REDENTOR, CRISTIANOS, NOS CONVIDA"

The Redeemer, Christians, invites us
To bewail his sorrowful passion;
With lively love let us shed our tears
For him who shed his blood for us.

To bewail his sorrowful passion
The Redeemer, Christians, invites us,
To bewail his sorrowful passion.
For him who shed his blood for us
With lively love let us shed our tears.

Who wove for him the crown of thorns?
Your folly, oh proud sinner,
Your vile self-will, your sensuality, your immodesty
Are the whips of his flagellation.

The Lord went out with his cross to the hill;
O sinner, you load him with the cross,
That deadly burden! which every day you make heavier
Pitilessly for the beautiful Jesus.

His lovely feet, his loving hands—
See the sharp nails pierce them.
My heart, do not prevent Jesus
From piercing you; be subject to his love.

Stretched on the cross between heaven and earth
The God-Man ransomed mankind;
He prayed for us to his heavenly Father,
And out of love gave us to his Mother.

O sinner, on Mount Calvary
Blush deep and raise your eyes
And contemplate what torment sin
Has made the God of holiness suffer.

With faith and sorrow, oh divine Lamb,
Subdue my heart to your feet;
May your blood wash its wickedness away:
By your cross, pardon us, Lord, pardon us!

EL REDENTOR, CRISTIANOS, NOS CONVIDA

El Redentor, cristianos, nos convida
Para llorar en su triste pasión:
Con vivo amor lágrimas tributemos
Al que por nos su sangre derramó.

**Para llorar en su triste pasión
El Redentor, cristianos, nos convida,
Para llorar en su triste pasión.
Al que por nos su sangre derramó
Con vivo amor lágrimas tributemos.**

¿Quién le ciñó la espinosa corona?
Tu insensatez, o vano pecador,
Tu vil placer, tu lujo, tu inmodestia
Azotes son de su flagelación:

Sale el Señor con el madero a cuestas:
O pecador, le cargaste la cruz,
¡Fardo fatal! que cada día aumentas
Sin compasión por el manso Jesús.

Sus bellos pies, sus benéficas manos
Los clavos ved, agudos, traspasar.
Mi corazón, a Jesús no resitas,
Con tanto amor déjate penetrar.

Suspenso en la cruz entre el cielo y la tierra
El Hombre Dios al hombre rescató,
Rogó por nos a su celestial Padre,
Y con amor a su Madre nos dió.

O pecador, en el Monte Calvario
Con gran rubor los ojos levantad,
Y contemplad qué suplicio el pecado
Hace sufrir al Dios de Santidad.

Con fe y dolor, o divino Cordero,
A vuestros pies rindo mi corazón;
De su maldad lávelo vuestra sangre:
Por vuestra cruz ¡perdón, Señor, perdón!

Upon arriving at the front of the church, the people line up on one side and the other, forming various groups until the statues, the banners, the priest, the servers, and the choir have entered. Then all the people go inside.

Within the church before the main altar are three tables to hold the statues. Jesus Christ is placed in the center, the Most Holy Virgin on the south side and Saint John on the north. The flowers and the crown of thorns are placed at the feet of Jesus Christ. The Mass of Easter Sunday follows.

AN EASTER SUNDAY SERMON
BY THE REVEREND FATHER JOSE ASSENMACHER
NINE IN THE MORNING—EASTER SUNDAY

In the name of the Father and of the Son and of the Holy Spirit, amen.

"He is risen! Praise be to God!"

The Church tell us to say, "Praise the Lord, Alleluia!"

The passion was not the whole story; the resurrection was more important. History shows it to us; there are many proofs.

The Pascal celebrations have always been the most important feast of the year. The Jews recognized this. The Holy Family went to Jerusalem with the Christ Child for it. The Jews celebrated this day because God had freed them from slavery, and the Christians have incorporated the Old Testament into the New, which has freed us from sin. Our Lord did not wish to take revenge upon his enemies, but only to triumph over sin.

"I am the resurrection and the eternal life."

According to Saint Paul, the resurrection of Christ is the assurance of our redemption; his resurrection was the resurrection of our own life in the form of an exemplar. The suffering of Our Lord on the cross was the sign of his victory; today he is risen, glorious and triumphant.

God created man in his own image and likeness, and he came into being free from death. But now from the moment a creature is born, death claims him, for the world is only a vale of tears.

And furthermore, Mary Most Holy suffered beneath the cross, witnessing the death of Our Lord for those who would believe. Mary Most Holy in her solitude knew that a day, two days, would pass, and that on the third day Jesus would rise,

Al llegar al frente de la iglesia, la gente se afila a un lado y otro formando varias filas hasta que pasan las estatuas, las banderas, el sacerdote y los sacristanes y el coro. Despues entra toda la gente.

Adentro de la iglesia delante del altar major hay tres mesas para poner las estatuas. Jesucristo queda en medio. La Santisima Virgen al lado sur Y San Juan al lado norte. Se depositan las flores y las espinas a los pies de Jesucristo. Sigue la Misa del Domingo de Pascuas.

SERMON DEL DOMINGO DE RESURRECCION POR EL REVERENDO PADRE JOSE ASSENMACHER TIEMPO—DOMINGO DE RESURRECCION A LAS 9:00 DE LA MANANA

En el nombre del Padre y del Hijo y del Espiritu Santo Amen.

"Resucito! Alabemos a Dios!"

La Iglesia nos dice, "Alabemos a Dios, Aleluya!"

La Pasion no fue todo, la resurreccion fue de mayor importancia. La historia nos prueba esto. Hay tantas pruebas.

Las celebraciones de Pascuas siempre fue la mas grande fiesta del ano. Los Judios le reconocieron. La Sagrada Familia con el Santo Nino estuvieron en Jerusalem. Los Judios celebravan este dia para que los librara Dios de la esclavitud, y los Cristianos han encorporado el viejo testamento al nuevo, el cual los ha librado del pecado. Nuestro Senor no quizo vengarse con sus enemigos. El triunfo contra el pecado.

"Yo soy la resurreccion y la vida eterna!"

San Pablo dijo que la resurreccion de Senor es la garantia de nuestro redemcio y que la resurreccion es de nuestra vida ejemplar. El tormento de nuestro Senor en la cruz fue senal de la victoria. Ahora resucito glorioso y triunfante.

Dios crio al hombre semejante a El, y nadie esta libre de la muerte. Desde el momento que la criatura nace ya la muerte lo aclama, porque este mundo solo es un valle de lagrimas.

No es todo, Maria Santisima sufrio vajo la cruz, presenciando la muerte de Nuestro Senor, por los fieles. Maria Santisima en su soledad sabia que pasarian un dia, dos dias y al

and that then she would be no more a Sorrowful Mother but the glorious Queen of Heaven.

If we ourselves wish to rise again, follow his example. If we wish to triumph we must take up the cross. Not by striking our breast and saying "Lord! Lord!" will we enter heaven, but by living in a Christian manner. We are going to win for ourselves either an eternal and glorious life or a life of tears. Live as the faith has taught us. Suffer! There can be no glory without serving others, there can be no eternal life without suffering. As Jesus Christ suffered for us, so we should suffer as well; and afterwards, Alleluia! Alleluia! and we shall triumph with him in life everlasting.

In the name of the Father and of the Son and of the Holy Spirit, amen.

* * *

When the Mass is over, the traditional ceremonies are concluded, as is Holy Week in Tomé. May God grant us life and health to return again next year.

tercer dia Jesus iba a resucitar y entonces ya ella no iba a ser una Madre Dolorosa sino gloriosa la Reina del cielo.

Si nosotros querremos resucitar, seguir su ejemplo. Si querremos triunfar debemos triunfar llevando la cruz. No con glopiarnos el pecho y decir Senor! Senor! vamos a entrar al cielo, sino vivir cristianamente. Vamos a ser vencedores entre una vida eterna y gloriosa o una vida de lagrimas. Vivir segun la fe nos ensena. Padecer! No hay gloria sin servir, no hay vida eterna sin padecer. Como Jesucristo padecio por nosotros asi debemos nosotros tambien padecer y luego, aleluya! Aleluya! triunfar como El en una vida eterna.

En el nombre del Padre y del Hijo y del Espiritu Santo Amen.

*   *   *

Con La Santa Misa termina el Deposito y tambien Semana Santa en Tomé. Dios nos preste vida y salud para volver otra vez el proximo año.

Poster for the Movie
and Mr. Otero's Narrative

VISTA MOVIBLE
Semana Santa
EN TOME
Ensenando el Drama
de la
Pasion y Muerte de Nuestro
SENOR JESUCRISTO
Por Primera vez ensenando en

_____

_____

Fecha

A Beneficio de la Iglesia Catolica de Tome

HOLY WEEK IN TOME

We dedicate this movie with affectionate gratitude to the present pastor and to all those persons who year by year have kept this religious tradition alive; to all those persons who up to the present exerted themselves to preserve these beautiful and meritorious works; to all those persons who took some part among the various characterizations; and finally to every good Catholic who strives to spend Holy Week in Tomé.

* * *

The representation of the passion and death of Our Lord Jesus Christ takes place in the Catholic Church of the Immaculate Conception in Tomé, New Mexico, Valencia County. Since 1781 when the church was built,[43] every year the ritual has been repeated in Tomé.

This year the dramatization begins on Holy Thursday. Since everything is in mourning, the bells of the church are not rung, and instead the servers use matracas—clackers—to summon the people.

The various pious families of Tomé, as well as those of the many neighboring communities, hasten to come by foot, or however they can, to commemorate the passion and death of Our Lord Jesus Christ, and to adore the holy name of him who died nailed to the cross to save men from sin.

It is remarkable that no written instructions are available concerning the program of these ceremonies, but they have been passed from generation to generation, notwithstanding some changes, until finally they have come down to us such as we see them today.

It is the wish of the present Society of Saint Joseph of Tomé to preserve these ceremonies, both for their spiritual value and for the picturesque and religious atmosphere brought about by these sermons and ceremonies so in keeping with our faith.

In this scene, we see Esteban Torrez, filling in for Julian Zamora, a revered actor in these services for many years, congratulating the present president of the Society of Saint Joseph, Fred Landavazo, and at the same time asking him to continue and augment these religious services and foster them to the full extent of his ability so that they do not die out.

---

43 The church was completed in 1750 and the services were first mentioned in 1776.

194

SEMANA SANTA EN TOME

Dedicamos esta obra con afectuosa gratitud al presente Reverende a todas aquellas personas quienes ano tras ano han revivido esta costumbre religiosa. A todas aquellas personas quienes aun ahora se esmeran pare preservar estos hermosos y effectivos oficios. A todos aquellas personas quienes toman parte en las diversas representaciones, y por fin a todo buen Catolico quien se esmera a pasar Semana Santa en Tome.

*   *   *

Esta escena de la pasion y muerte de nuestro Senor Jesucristo toma lugar en la iglesia Catolica de la Inmaculada Concepcion de Tome, Nuevo Mejico, Condado de Valencia. Desde 1781 cuando esta iglesia fue construida, anualmente se ha acostumbrado deposito en Tome.

Este ano se ha empezado esta escena el Jueves Santo. Como todo está en luto, no se repican las campanas de la iglesia, sino se usan matracas por los sacristanes para llamar a la gente.

Las diferentes familias religiosas de Tome, como tambien de las diferentes comunidades vecindarias, se dan lugar para venir ya sea a pie, o de otra manera, a revivar sus recuerdos de la pasion y muerte de nuestro Senor Jesucristo, y adorar el Santo nombre de aquel que murio clavado en la cruz para salvarlos del pecado.

Lo mas curioso es que no se encuentra nada escrito acerca del procedimiento de estos ejercicios, sino que se han ido pasando de generacion a generacion, no obstante con algunos cambios, hasta por fin llegar a nosotros tal como los vemos ahora.

Son los deseos de la presente Sociedad de San Jose de Tomé, de preservar estos costumbres, tanto por su valor espiritual, como por el ambiente religioso y pintoresco causados por estos ejercicios, sermones, y oficios tan armoniosos con nuestra creencia.

En este saludo, representamos a Estevan Torrez, actuando por Julian Zamora, anciano actor de dichos servicios por muchos anos, congratulando al presente presidente de la Sociedad de San Jose, Fred Landavazo, y al mismo tiempo pidiendole que continuen y engrandescan dichos servicios religiosos y los desarrollen a lo mejor de su capacidad, para que no mueran.

All the persons who take part in the offices and active parts, such as the priest, the servers, the Roman soldiers, the Jews and their leader, as well as those who direct and safeguard good order, are local talent. They help out because they are naturally helpful, or they have made a promise of some sort, or just for the enjoyment of helping.

The scene this year begins on Holy Thursday, when the leader of the Jews joins with his people to do away with Jesus of Nazareth, accusing him of being a false prophet, and handing him over to the judgment of Pontius Pilate, at that time the prefect of Palestine.

The First Station: The second scene takes place at the front of the church, in the palace of Pilate. When the case was presented, Pilate saw that the accused man was not guilty, and said, "Jesus of Nazareth is innocent; I find no guilt at all in this man." The leader of the Jews cries, "He is an enemy of Caesar, a disturber of public order and a spreader of false teaching."

After Pilate has let Barabbas go, he washes his hands and says, "I am innocent of the blood of this just man."

And Jesus is condemned to death.

The Second Station: This is where our beloved Jesus raises onto his wounded shoulders the heavy weight of the cross.

The Third Station: Our Lord, climbing up toward Calvary with the cross, groaning and sighing, falls to the ground under the holy cross for the first time.

The Fourth Station: Our Lord, journeying toward Calvary with the holy cross, encounters his most holy mother in her sadness and affliction.

The Fifth Station: The Jews enlist Simon of Cyrene and with threats force him to help carry the cross. They are not motivated by mercy but by fear that Jesus will die on the way from the burden of the cross.

The Sixth Station: The woman Veronica, seeing Jesus so tired and with his face covered with perspiration, dust, spittle, and blood from the abuse he received, wipes his face with her veil. Then she shows the cloth to the bystanders with the countenance of the Lord imprinted on it.

The Seventh Station: The holy women of Jerusalem encounter the Lord and weep bitterly to see him so badly hurt.

The Eighth Station: Jesus falls for the second time beneath the cross in front of the door to the courthouse. Jesus has sustained a large and deadly wound in his shoulder.[44]

44 *Note the change of the usual order, where the second fall is the Seventh Station.*

Las personas que toman parte en los oficios y representaciones, como son el sacerdote, los sacristanes, los soldados Romanos, los Judios y su jefe, como tambien los que dirigen y guardan el buen orden, son talento local. Estos ayudan porque les ha nacido ayudar, o ya sea por alguna promesa, o por el gusto de servir.

La escena este ano empieza el Jueves Santo, cuando el jefe de los Judios junta a su gente para llevar a Jesus Nazareno, acusado como falso profeta, delente del juicio de Poncio Pilato, en ese tiempo Presidente de la Inferior Galilea.

Primera Estacion: La segunda escena toma lugar delante de la iglesia en la casa de Pilato. Al presentar la causa, Pilato ve que aquel acusado no tiene culpa y dice: "Jesus de Nazareno es inocente." "No hayo culpa alguna en este hombre." El jefe de los Judios grita: "Es el enemigo del Cesar, inquietador de las Republicas y sembrador de doctrinas falsas."

Pilato despues de soltar a Barrabas, lavandose las manos dice: "Inocente soy de la sangre de este justo."

Jesus es sentenciado a muerte.

Segunda Estacion: Aqui es donde nuestro amado Jesus le pusieron en sus lastimados hombros el grave peso de la cruz.

Tercera Estacion: El senor caminando a cuestas con la cruz, gimiendo y suspirando, cayo en tierra y debajo de la santa cruz por primera vez.

Cuarta Estacion: Caminando el senor con la santa cruz a cuestas, se encuentra con su santisima madre triste y afligida.

Quinta Estacion: Los Judios alquilaron a Simon Sirineo y a arrempujones lo hacen ayudar con la cruz. No movidos de piedad, sino temiendo que Jesus se muriere en el camino por el peso de la cruz.

Sexta Estacion: La mujer Veronica viendo a Jesus tan fatigado, y su rostro obscurecido por el sudor, el polvo, saliva y bofetadas que le habien dado, con su lienzo le limpia el rostro. Despues muestra el lienzo al publico y el senor esta impreso en el.

Septima Estacion: Las piadosas mujeres de Jerusalem encuentran al senor y lloran amargamente de verle tan injuriado.

Octava Estacion: Jesus cae por segunda vez bajo la cruz. El lugar es la puerta judiciaria. A Jesus se le ha hecho una llaga muy grande y mortal en su hombro.

The Ninth Station: Jesus falls beneath the cross for the third time, falling to the ground so that he lies with his sacred mouth against the dirt. Attempting to rise, he cannot, and falls again.

The congregation listens attentively to the sermon about the three falls preached by the pastor of Tomé, the Reverend José Assenmacher.

The Tenth Station: Now that the Lord has arrived at Mount Calvary, he is stripped of his garments. They nail him to the cross, and in his agony offer him to drink wine mixed with myrrh. In accordance with the decree of Pilate, he has been crucified between two thieves, Dismas and Gestas, by both of whom he is consoled until his death.

The Jews dispose of the holy robe of Jesus by casting dice.

Joseph and Nicodemus take the body down from the cross, and Nicodemus takes him in his arms and gives him to his most holy mother. They wrap him in a winding sheet. Two women cleanse his face of the blood. He is embalmed and placed in the coffin and carried to the Holy Sepulchre. The lining of the coffin is silk; the coffin is covered with fresh flowers. After he is placed in the coffin, the people put perfume on him. During this procession, five stops are made to symbolize the five wounds of Our Lord.

The centurion, at this time, also wears mourning.

At the end of the various services, it has been a very ancient custom for the people of the congregation to stay for some minutes outside the church, greeting one another and discussing the problems of the community, whether social or agricultural or their various interests.

The Holy Saturday services are inside the church and are followed by those of Easter Sunday.

Singing "Alleluia," the men file out of the church and make one group on the plaza, carrying the Redeemer who has arisen from the dead, and in another group walk the women with his most holy mother. Saint John, elated with joy, runs to carry the news to Mary most holy of the resurrection of her son. With the same joy he runs back and forth. The meeting between Jesus and Mary most holy, his mother, moves the heart of every Christian. For ourselves, this is the most important moment in the whole drama, for it gives proof that Jesus Christ and his teachings have triumphed in the end. With a harmonious sound, the church bells announce the resurrection of the Redeemer of the world.

With the holy Mass after this procession, the ceremony comes to an end, as does Holy Week in Tomé. May God grant all the people life and health to return next year.

Novena Estacion: Jesus cae bajo la cruz por tercera vez en tierra, hasta llegar con su santa boca en el suelo. Queriendose levantar, no puede y cae de nuevo.

La congregacion escucha atentamente el sermon de las tres caidas, por el presente Reverendo de Tome, su altesa, Jose Assenmacher.

Decima Estacion: Habiendo llegado el senor al Monte Calvario, lo desnudaron. Lo clavaron en la cruz, y en su agonia le dieron a beber vino mesclado con hiel. En acuerdo con el decreto de Pilato, fue crucificado entre dos landrones, Dimas y Gestas. A quienes consolo hasta en la muerte.

Los Judios disponen de la santa ropa de Jesus con tirar dados.

Jose y Nicodemos lo abajan de la cruz y Nicodemos lo toma en sus brazos y se lo presenta a su santisima madre. Lo hechan en una sabana. Dos senoras limpian la sangre de su rostro. Es embalsamado y puesto en una urna, lo llevan al santo sepulcro. La cama en la urna es de seda. La urna esta cubierta de flores frescas. Despues de ser puesto en la urna la gente le hecha perfume. Durante esta procesion, hay cinco paradas que representan las cinco llagas de nuestro senor.

El Cinturion en este dia tambien se viste de luto.

Al terminar los diferentes servicios, ha sido costumbre muy antigua que los de la congregacion se paren por unos minutos afuera de la iglesia, a saludarse, o discutir problemas de comunidad, ya sean sociales, agricolas, o de sus diferentes intereses.

Los servicios del sabado de gloria son dentro de la iglesia y sigue los del domingo de resurreccion.

Cantando "Alleluiah" los hombres salen en fila pur un lado de la plaza con el redentor resucitado, y por el otro lado las mujeres con su santisima madre. San Juan regocigando de gusto corre a traer las nuevas a Maria santisima, de la resurreccion de su hijo. Del mismo gusto corre para tras y para adelante. El encuentro de Jesus y Maria santisima, su madre, mueve el corazon de todo cristiano. Para nosotros, este es el momento mas importante de esta escena, porque da a pruebas que Jesucristo y su doctrina han reinado en el fin. Con armonioso sonido las campanas de la iglesia anuncian la resurreccion del redentor del mundo.

Con la santa misa despues de esta procesion, el deposito y semana santa en Tome termina. Que Dios los preste vida y salud para volver otra vez el proximo ano.

ADDENDA: Two other versions of "La Sentencia"

A scenario from about 1950.

SENTENCIA DE JESUS

Yo Poncio Pilatos Presidente de la inferior Galilea; Hoy dia 25 de Marzo de le ano 5,001 De la creacion del mundo mando y sentencio a Jesus llamado por el pueblo Nazareno, que sea crucificado en una cruz y puesto entre dos ladrones, Dimas y Gestas ya sentenciados a muerte el uno a la diestra y el otro a la fasiniestra en el monte llamado Gorgota como falso profeta enganador de las gentes inquietador de las republicas sembrador de doctrinas falsas y Negromatico; que compacta con los demonios, obra finjidos milagros, valiendose de Belzebub, Principe del Infierno, y como tirano usurpador de reinos y traidor al Cesar Emperador de los Romanos; y tambien mando a nuestro Senturion quinto Cornelio que lo pasee en todas las calles de Jerusalem con un pregonero que vaya gritando todas las maldades del Reo para que sirva a todo el pueblo, y pasara por la puerta judiciaria donde sera leida aqui mi sentencia, ademas ordeno que sea puesto un rotulo arriva de la cruz que reze asi;
"Jesus Nazareno Rey de Los Judios!"
El cual sera escrito en tres idiomas; Erbraica, Griega y Latina esto es para que todos la puedan leer, y entender.

Esta es nuestra voluntad hecha y firmada en la fecha arriba mencionada en nuestro Palacio.

Poncio Pilatos, Presidente

THE SENTENCE OF DEATH READ BY PONTIUS PILATE IN TOME PASSION PLAY

Yo Poncio Pilató, presidente de la inferior Galilea, hoy dia 25 de marzo del ano 5001 de la creacion del mundo, mando y sentencio a Jesús, llamado por el pueblo, Nazareno, que sea crucificado en una cruz y puesto entre dos ladrones, Dimas y Gestas ya sentenciados a muerte, el uno a la diestra y el otro a la siniestra en el monte llamado Gólgata, como falso profeta, engañador de las gentes, inquietador de las republicas, sembrador de doctrinas falsas, y negromántico, que con pacto

A SCENARIO FROM ABOUT 1950

The Lord in Prison: Sermon

The Roman soldiers guard Jesus in the prison. During the sermon, three little angels come to sweep the cell and offer Christ flowers, perfumes, and incense. After the sermon the congregation prays the Holy Rosary and they all sing "Pues Padeciste por Amor Nuestro."

Good Friday in the morning:

The prophecies, the prayers, the psalms, and the adoration of the Most Holy Cross. Then the procession goes out to pray the stations of the Way of the Cross. Choir and congregation sing, all walking with proper fervor, respect, order, and reverence. The first Station takes place in front of the church: The balcony is the palace of Pontius Pilate. With him are some guards of honor and other soldiers. A boy waits on him. Barabbas is there with a soldier to guard him. The choir sings the first stanza of "Acompañemos al Calvario—O Cristianos." Then they sing the stanza "O Jesus la Mortal Sententia,"[45] and finally the priest reads the first station.

---

45 The stanza of "Acompañemos al Calvario" which narrates the first station of the Way of the Cross.

con los demónios obra fingidos milagros, valiéndose para ello de Beelzebub, príncipe del infierno, y como tirano usurpador de reinos, y traidor al César emperador de los romanos. Y tambien mando a nuestro centurión, Quinto Cornelio, que lo pasee en todas las calles de Jerusalén con un pregonero que vaya gritando todas las maldades del reo, para que sirva de ejemplo a todo el pueblo, y pasará por la puerta judiciaria, donde será leida aquí mi sentencia. Además ordeno que sea puesto un rétulo arriba de la cruz que reze asi: Jesús Nazareno Rey de los Judios, el cual rétulo será escrito en tres idiomas, hebraica, griega, y latina. Esta es nuestra voluntad.

Hecho y firmado en la fecha arriba mencionada en nuestro palacio, paraque todos lo puedan leer y entender.

Poncio Pilato, presidente
(18 nov. 1905)

El Senor en la Carcel: Sermon

Los Soldados Romanos velan a Jesus en la carcel. Durante el sermon vienen tres Angelistos a barrer la Carcel, ofrecer flores, perfumes Y encienso. Terminado el sermon la gente resa el Santo Rosario Y todos cantan PUES PADECISTE POR AMOR NUESTRO.

Viernes Santo en la Manana:

A las & las profesias, officios, Salmos Y adoracion de la Santissima Cruz. En seguida sale la procession resando las estanciones del Via Crucis. El coro Y gente cantan—todas van con el debido fervor, respecto, orden, Y reverencia. La primera Estacion toma lugar frente a la iglesia: El Balcon es la casa de Poncio Pilato. Con este estan algunos guardias de Honor y otros Soldados. Un nino le sirve a Pilato. Barrabas Y en soldadio lo vela, El coro canta: ACOMPANEMOS AL CALVARIO—O CRISTIANOS. En seguida cantan: O HESUS LA MORTAL SENTENCIA, y en seguida el Padre resa la primera estacion.

Pilate: Jesus of Nazareth is innocent; I find no guilt at all in this man.

Leader: He is guilty. Condemn him to the cross!

Jews: To the cross! Condemn him to the cross! To the cross (etc; they cry out at length).

Leader: He is an enemy of Caesar! He is a disturber of the republic, a deceiver of the people, and a spreader of false doctrines!

Jews: To the cross! (etc.) Let him die by crucifixion!

Pilate: Whom do you wish me to release, Jesus, the innocent, gentle, good, and just man, or this despicable man, this lawbreaker, this criminal Barabbas?

Leader: Destroy the life of Jesus and set Barabbas free!

Jews: Long live Barabbas! (etc.)

Here Pilate gives the order to a soldier who removes the chains from the criminal and hangs them over the balcony railing in sight of all the people; Barabbas cries "Liberty!" and goes to join the Jews, who all cry, "Viva—Viva Barabbas!"

Pilate: I am innocent of the blood of this just man. (Lavabo Manus Meas) (He washes his hands)

Leader: Let his blood fall upon us and upon our children!

Pilate: I Pontius Pilate (etc.; he reads the Sentence).

Pilate: We here declare forfeit the emblem of this condemned man. (Now a soldier breaks the token, a small staff. Another soldier places the sentence on the centurion's lance, and he leads the procession with a great show of ceremony. The priest follows, reading the stations of the Way of the Cross; all the ceremonies and tableaux take the order given by the Way of the Cross. The director and Leader is Don Estevan Torrez. Many persons help him as he appointed them to. At the end of the Ninth Station the priest gives the sermon.)

After the tenth, the Jews and the Roman soldiers throw dice to try to win the clothing of Jesus.

Good Friday in the afternoon: If the weather is good this sermon takes place at the Memorial Monument.

The Jews and Romans assemble inside and enter in order; the priest gives the sermon; when the temple veil is torn open all fall on their knees and sing "Perdón O Dios Mío." Then the

Pilato: Jesus de Nazareno es innocente, Yo no hallo culpa alguna en este hombre.

Jefe: Es culpable—condenalo a La Cruz!

Judios: ¡A La Cruz! Condenalo a La Cruz! A La Cruz, (etc.; gritan mucho).

Jefe: Es el enemigo de Cesar, inquitador de las republicas enganador de las gentes Y sembrador de doctrinas falsas!

Judios: A La Cruz! (etc.) Que muera Crucificado!

Pilato: A quien quereis; A Jesus el hobre innocente, el manso, el bueno, el Justo, O a este hobre vil, este reo, el criminal Barrabas?

Jefe:¡Quitale a Jesus la vida Y sueltanos (entrieganos) libre a Barrabas!

Judios: ¡Viva Barrabas! (etc.)

Aqui Pilato manda a un soldado Y este le quita las cadenas al reo Y las cuelga del balcon a vista de todo el pueblo, Y barrabas grita "Libertad" Y viene a juntarse con los Judios Y todos gritan "Viva—Viva—Barrabas".

Pilato: Innocente (Y soy innocente) soy de la Sangre de este Justo (Lavabo Manus Meas) (Se lava las Manos).

Jefe: Que Caiga Su Sangre sobre nosotros Y sobre nuestros Hijos!

Pilato: Yo, Poncio Pilato (etc.)-(La Sentencia)

Pilato: Tomamos aqui el Baston de este condenado. (Aqui un soldado quiebra el baston. Otro soldado pone la sentencia en la lanza del centurion Y este se va adelante de la procession con Brio Y Bompa. Sigue el Padre resando las estaciones del Via Crucis Y todas las ceremonias Y representaciones estan en el orden segun el Via Crucis. El director Y Jefe es Don Estevan Torrez. Mucha gente le ayuda segun este les nombra. Al fin de la Novena estacion el Padre dice su sermon.)

Despues de la Decima los Judios Y soldados Romanos Juegan para quedarse con el vestido de Jesus.

Viernes Santo en la Tarde: Si el tiempo esta bueno este sermon tomara lugar en el Monumento Memorial.

Los Judios Y Romanos se reunen en el cuartel Y entran en orden—el Padre dice su sermon y Cuando se rompre el velo del templo todos caen de rodillas y cantan PERDON O DIOS MIO.

procession of the Holy Body goes out, with the priest and choir singing "Miserere Mei Deus." Five times they venerate and worship (using incense) the five wounds of the Savior. During the procession the people bring their missals and rosaries forward, and the good Jews and Romans touch them to the Sacred Wounds of the Lord.

Good Friday in the evening:

The sermon and procession of Our Lady of Solitude. All sing "Ayudemos Almas," "Stabat Mater Dolorosa," and "Al Pie de un tosco leño."[46]

46 An alternate name for "Venid Almas Devotas."

En seguida sale la procession del Santo Cuerpo—Y el Padre y coro cantan MISERERE MEI DEUS. Se veneran y adoran Cinco veces (con incienso) las cinco Llegas Del Salvador. Durante la procession la Gente lleva sus libros Y rosarios, Y los Buenos Judios Y Romanos les retocan en las Sagradas Llegas del Senor.

Viernes Santo en La Noche.

Sermon y procession de Nuestra Senora de La Soledad. Todos cantan AYUDEMOS ALMAS, Y STABAT MATER DOLOROSA, Y AL PIE DE UN TOSCO LENO.

www.ingramcontent.com/pod-product-compliance
Lightning Source LLC
Chambersburg PA
CBHW032058080426
42733CB00006B/323